NATIVE AMERICAN HISTORY

Accurate & Comprehensive History, Origins, Culture, Tribes, Legends, Mythology, Wars, Stories & More of The Native Indigenous Americans

HISTORY BROUGHT ALIVE

FREE BONUS FROM HBA: EBOOK BUNDLE

Greetings!

First of all, thank you for reading our books. As fellow passionate readers of History and Mythology, we aim to create the very best books for our readers.

Now, we invite you to join our VIP list. As a welcome gift, we offer the History & Mythology Ebook Bundle below for free. Plus you can be the first to receive new books and exclusives! <u>Remember it's 100% free to join.</u>

Scan the QR code to join.

Keep up to date with us on:

YouTube: History Brought Alive

Facebook: History Brought Alive

www.historybroughtalive.com

CONTENTS

CONTENTS

INTRODUCTION

We are fortunate to live in a modern world with information at our fingertips. With all the information available, it's surprising that when it comes to history topics, including the history of Indigenous Peoples in North America, the resources we find tend to be dry and dull like an old-fashioned encyclopedia. Frequently, history books are written by academics for academics and are too nuanced or in-depth to capture the curiosity and imagination of the average reader. These history books fail to pique the interests of average people who want to

1

learn more about historical times or cultures.

History Brought Alive strives to deliver history books that everyone will enjoy. History Brought Alive offers a series of history books thoughtfully inspired by you, our reader, and all the people of the world. In this book, we will educate you about the history of Indigenous Peoples in North America. We believe that we build more understanding and respect through education and awareness. We do this by offering you a book that is well researched and laid out in a way that flows from one topic to the next to build on what you're learning. We say "goodbye!" to old-school history texts and invite you to enjoy learning and expanding your knowledge on this subject.

Multiculturalism

Another incredible feature of this modern-day world is the extent to which accessible travel and globalism have brought us all together. We now live in a multicultural world and interact with many more cultures and people than ever before. For this reason, it is essential to learn more about cultures beyond your own. Education builds awareness, understanding, and compassion. Learning more about different cultures and histories is a part of being a good global citizen. Whether you travel frequently or not you probably come into contact with dozens of people of various backgrounds and cultures every day without even realizing it. Learning more about history allows for deeper conversations and understanding of everyone around us. It helps us to be more inclusive and less judgmental when it comes to other cultures.

Era of Reconciliation

At this point in history, it is essential for people to learn more about the history of Indigenous Peoples in North America. Tragically, and for far too long, the various Indigenous cultures in North America have been systematically eliminated, misrepresented, and misunderstood. Poor historical treatment has led to deeply seeded trauma and adverse economic and health outcomes for many Indigenous People. Recently, there has been more information available about the mistreatment of Indigenous People and the intergenerational effects of that mistreatment. Some of the adverse impacts for people of Indigenous descent include higher rates of poverty, children in state care, shorter life expectancy, and higher rates of drug or alcohol substance use disorders. These outcomes are related to the experience of trauma and poverty and become compounded with multigenerational trauma, such as experienced by most Indigenous People.

We are at the brink of a decisive turning point in North America, where people can share an

Indigenous perspective more broadly through social media and other alternative news sources and narratives. The broader ability to share information has opened many more eyes to the racism, injustices, and challenges Indigenous people have faced since colonialism. It is a point at which we all need to take responsibility to become educated about the long history and diverse cultures of Native Americans and begin to develop an awareness of how colonialism and continued colonial practices affect present-day Indigenous people and culture.

We hope that everyone may support the future generations of Indigenous Peoples in healing and grow into a beautiful new Era through education and understanding. This book is an excellent starting place for your learning journey and understanding the complex history of Indigenous Peoples in North America. Begin here with "The Complete History of Indigenous Peoples in North America" but we urge you to dive deeper into the local history in the area you inhabit. We would also encourage you to seek out Indigenous-owned and curated businesses, shops, apparel, art, and literature in your local area. Each part of the continent is home to a distinct and diverse Native American nation or tribe, so it's a good idea to learn about the history specific to your area to understand the people around you better.

Land Acknowledgement

We wish to acknowledge and honor that we live and work on the ancestral lands and traditional territories of many Indigenous tribes and nations across North America.

As we will discuss in detail later in this book, everything changed for Indigenous Peoples when European colonizers arrived to settle in North America. Before colonization, Indigenous peoples lived sustainably with the environment and had no reason to change their traditional ways of life for thousands of years. Only when colonizers arrived in present-day North America, was their sustainable way of life disrupted.

The colonizers destroyed the subtle balance that existed between humans and the environment for tens of thousands of years. Colonizers were ignorant and didn't understand the connection that Indigenous Peoples had to the land and how they relied on it to live nor how it was tied to their beliefs and traditions. As Indigenous Peoples were forced off of traditional territories or onto small reserves of land in the territories, they could no longer live sustainably, and many poor outcomes have resulted.

At the same time, as Indigenous people were being negatively affected by displacement and limited land usage due to colonialism, the settling colonizers were directly profiting from it. The culture clash between greedy colonizers and holistic Indigenous peoples caused a drastic imbalance in the power dynamic. Today, this still affects the relationship between settler descendants and Indigenous people in North America. It took a few hundred years before people in the dominant culture started to clearly see how much colonialism has affected Indigenous people.

At this point in history in North America, more and more people are showing respect by acknowledging the heritage of the land and of the people who lived on it for thousands of years. This new practice is called Land Acknowledgement. It is now common to hear or read a Land Acknowledgement at the beginning of many events and gatherings, on business websites, or through literature from non-profit organizations. Land Acknowledgements serve to honor true history by recognizing the historical fact that European colonizers stole Indigenous Peoples' land in North America.

CHAPTER 1

A BRIEF HISTORY OF HUMANITY

Before we dig into the vibrant history of

the Indigenous Peoples in North America, we will take a trip back in time, about 2 million years. It would be hard to begin the story of Indigenous Peoples without first briefly touching on the history of the evolution of humans and where we first appeared, and how and when we migrated across the globe. This way, we can put into context the arrival of

Indigenous Peoples in North America. Recounting the evolution of humanity is also a way to remind us all that we are a united race with a common ancestral beginning. Since the dawn of humanity, people have dispersed into different parts of the world; that dispersion has led to so many diverse and beautiful human cultures.

Prehistoric Human Ancestors

Although scientists are still unsure exactly when and where humans first came into existence, the earliest human ancestor remains were discovered in the country now known as Kenya and are dated to be nearly 3 million years old. Every time another ancient prehistoric artifact is uncovered, it brings new information and insight. Because of this, we will likely never know for sure the precise origins of the human race.

For some of us, the idea of our own species' origin remaining a mystery is frustrating or confusing; for many scientists, this is what makes anthropology and paleontology so interesting. Scientists and anthropologists who work on these types of excavations are constantly motivated by the quest to solve the mystery and uncover the next fossil that will unlock another aspect of ancient humanity and fill in some gaps of our origin story.

Because it wasn't until about 5,000 years ago that humans began to maintain records, other than verbally communicated memories and information, we rely heavily on the information discovered from fossils and ancient relics. Anthropologists use that information to continuously piece together an idea of how and where ancient humans lived, what they ate, and where they traveled.

Modern-day humans are a part of the Hominini family of primates, which the Merriam-Webster dictionary defines as: "any of a taxonomic tribe (Hominini) of hominids that includes recent humans together with extinct ancestral related forms." Due to the availability of genetic testing from ancient samples, we know there were several species of archaic humans, such as Neanderthals and different types of hominids. It is also now known that many of these species were close enough to mate and produce offspring and continue human evolution in that way. Our species, the Homo sapiens, directly evolved from the Homo erectus, which coupled with other species such as Neanderthals. The outcome of all this means that we modern-day humans have genes from many now-extinct human species.

Each of these human ancestors had distinct features, abilities, and lifestyles; they each played a part in forming our modern species of humans, the Homo sapiens. The earliest remains and evidence of the existence of Homo sapiens specifically, were also found in the eastern region of Africa near Kenya and Ethiopia and dated from around 315,000 years ago. Of all the types of *hominids* that existed over millions of years, modern humans or Homo sapiens are the only ones that remain. Our closest living relatives who still exist are primates such as gorillas and orangutans.

Migration of Prehistoric Humans

The geographical world and environment of the ancient hominid species were vastly different from our world today, including the physical placement and locations of the continents and land on Earth. Scientists currently believe that when hominids were first evolving, all the continents on the planet were bunched together into one giant landmass called Pangea. The connected landmass of Pangea eventually separated and moved into the locations we have today by the slow and continuous drifting of the continental plates. The continental plates continue to drift to this day at a prolonged and imperceptible rate. This continental drift created many of the beautiful natural features in our world today, including the collision of tectonic plates that caused mountains to form.

Evidence suggests that human ancestors existed on the continent now known as Africa for about 1 million years before migrating eastward through present-day Europe and beyond to what is now known as Asia. The oldest hominid remains in Asia are a pair of teeth found in China, dating from about 1.7 million years ago. There has been other evidence of Homo erectus found in China that dates back even further. It's safe for scientists to say that our ancient ancestors had made it from Africa to Asia about 2 million years ago.

Remains and artifacts in Europe date the arrival and habitation of hominids in that area around 600,000 years ago. However, it is not believed that Homo sapiens were in Europe until about 45,000 years ago. Anthropologists do not know why Homo sapiens took so long to inhabit Europe. There is plenty of evidence that Homo sapiens had already been inhabiting Asia, which would have required them to pass through Europe from Africa to Asia, long before they finally inhabited Europe. Exactly when and why Homo sapiens finally populated Europe is a question that will require further archaeological discoveries to be able to answer.

CHAPTER 2
THEORIES OF ARRIVAL IN THE AMERICAS

Human arrival in the Americas is relatively recent compared with the rest of human evolution and migration history. Exactly when and how it happened remains somewhat mysterious, with ongoing discoveries changing the former theories and bringing up new likely scenarios of how the first Indigenous peoples may have arrived in the Americas. It is presumed that different groups of humans may have made their way here at other times and in different ways. This chapter will share the main western scientific theories of how people made their way to the Americas—followed in the next chapter by Indigenous origin stories and views.

The Bering Land Bridge Theory

Perhaps you are familiar with the Bering Land Bridge theory of how humans first migrated from Asia to the Americas. Until a few short years ago, when paleontologists discovered new artifacts, it was commonly believed and taught that humans first made their way to North America by following and hunting big game animals across a span of land that once existed between Alaska and Siberia. The previous evidence suggested that this happened about 13,000-14,000 years ago, where the Bering Strait exists today.

It was believed in this theory that as the ice receded after the Ice Age, a group of humans who had been inhabiting eastern Asia were able to cross a land bridge that became accessible for migration by foot. Although anthropologists widely accepted the Bering Land Bridge theory for many years, there always remained questions about whether it was possible given the age of the artifacts and the dates of the ice receding. It seemed that the evidence of humans in America was older than the time when the Bering Land Bridge would have been clear of ice. For that reason, scientists had been left seeking more information on when and how Indigenous People made their way to North America.

Beringia

It appears that what was called the Bering Land Bridge was a sizable continent-sized landmass now called Beringia. Twenty-five thousand years ago, that area was a massive and rare piece of dry land during the Ice Age. Due to unique natural conditions, it miraculously remained clear of ice despite the arctic conditions that enveloped the entire Earth at that time. Throughout the Ice Age, most of the Earth's water was in the form of glaciers and ice, making the world's water level much lower than it is today, allowing for more coastal land to be exposed. Because of that, Beringia connected the eastern side of Asia from Siberia to the western side of North America in the Alaska region.

A few pieces of land in the Bering Strait remain above water, and there has been evidence of mammoth bones and other fossils uncovered on those islands that suggest that humans were present there at least 25,000 years ago, not 14,000 as previously believed. These initial discoveries led scientists to question the timing of our human ancestors' first arrival in North America. As scientists broadened their search for artifacts into Alaska and Siberia, they have collected evidence of ancient human activity on either side of the Bering Strait. In Alaska, the artifacts are 20,000-25,000 years old, and on the Siberia side, they are over 35,000 years. Some evidence suggests that 25,000 years ago, the ice would not have been receded enough to be passable from Siberia to Alaska via the Bering Land Bridge; leading some scientists to believe that it is possible that Indigenous people were in that area for much, much longer than previously believed. This mounting evidence points to the fact that ancient humans actually inhabited that entire area for quite a long time. It is now recognized as having been an exceptional place and time in both history and geography, a unique place where the environment put humans' ability to survive to the test in extremely harsh conditions.

These are important discoveries that have altered the former theories of timeline and mode of the arrival of the Indigenous People in North America. Scientists believe the answers to many of these questions are encapsulated deep beneath the Bering Sea, a buried treasure from our ancestors.

The Clovis Culture People

For decades, the dominant theory of human population in the Americas was that ancient people crossed the Bering Land Bridge about 13,000 years ago. The theory held that the Indigenous People gradually migrated south from the Canadian far north down to South America. In the 1920s, archaeological remains of tools and bones found in Clovis, New Mexico, gave anthropologists the first views of the type of culture and lifestyle these Indigenous people had. They named this culture and the people after the site where the artifacts were discovered, the Clovis people. It was found that the Clovis people migrated to many parts of the Americas, and it was believed for a long time that they were the original gene source in North and South America.

Since the advancements and availability of genetic testing on ancient bone artifacts, scientists have been able to piece together more of the puzzle of the history of the Indigenous population of the Americas. However, some genetic test results have also raised questions about unknown gene sources linked to a previously unknown group of people who are not genetically related to the Clovis people. Another shocking discovery is that the gene lineage associated with the Clovis people seems to have ended abruptly around 9,000 years ago. This type of information and the insights that scientists have gained from it would never have been possible until a few years ago as technology advanced.

Here is an excerpt from the article *Clovis People Spread to Central and South America, then*

Vanished, which explains the impact of genetic testing and how it has informed anthropologists and altered views about ancient humans in North America:

Ancient DNA offered a new way to look at the question. Reich and his collaborators compared ancient peoples' genes from sites in Central and South America to genes from a Clovis-linked individual who lived in today's Montana between 12,700 and 12,900 years ago. There was a clear match between the Montana individual's genes and the three oldest genetic samples in the new study, which came from Chile, Brazil, and Belize. [...]

But then came the surprise. The great majority of the other individuals analyzed, who lived from Belize to Patagonia between 3,000 and 9,000 years ago, belonged to a different genetic lineage. The data imply that a population separate and distinct from the Clovis group also swept south from North America, largely replacing the Clovis-linked lineages. Their identity? Still a mystery. Reich is hoping that archeologists can help solve the puzzle, in combination with additional ancient DNA data. "That's an exciting part of the active dialogue between these two fields," he says. (Reich, 2018, para 7-9)

Another plot-twisting discovery came from testing samples that had been collected from across the Americas. During the testing process, scientists discovered a unique and distinct ancient human DNA from a sample found in South America, which is older than any Clovis DNA samples. This discovery points to the fact that there was or had already been a distinct human population in South America by the time the Clovis people reached it.

It now seems likely that the Clovis people migrating through the Bering Land Bridge is one of the ways that prehistoric humans came to North America, but it is unlikely that it is the only way. So, once again, as anthropologists gain more information, they are left with more questions. There is still no connection between the older South American DNA samples with any other known people, but scientists are hoping that one day a new sample will turn up to provide an answer.

The Kelp Highway

For many decades, anthropologists have considered the idea of prehistoric humans making their way to the Americas via sea as opposed to land. Until a few years ago, this idea was not held with much esteem but viewed as a peripheral possibility. More recently, due to the mounting evidence that proves that humans did inhabit the Americas before the Bering Land Bridge would have been clear of ice to facilitate passage, the idea of marine travel is becoming more popular. Many anthropologists now regard the theory of prehistoric maritime travel as the most likely way our ancient ancestors could have traveled when they did.

Although maritime travel now appears to be the most plausible way the very first humans arrived in the Americas, there is still very little known about how they did it. Anthropologists have long known that ancient humans were capable of maritime travel and had populated other regions, for example, Australia, in that way.

Maritime scientists, called paleoecologists, study ancient environments and the relationship between the environment and the people, plants, and animals of that time. They are investigating the Pacific coastline to better understand the type of marine and coastal environment that the ancient seafarers may have been navigating. Because the water level in the ocean was considerably lower at the time the ancient humans were traveling, it is believed that much of the evidence of their maritime travel and coastal lifestyle in the Americas is now underwater and most likely washed away or eroded. Anthropologists now view the submersion of the prehistoric coastline and the resulting loss of artifacts as a potential reason why they had not seriously evaluated this Kelp Highway Theory. Because of the inability to access the prehistoric coast, scientists are somewhat discouraged about the prospects of uncovering artifacts that can help fill in the details about the prehistoric maritime migration.

Islands along the pacific rim of North America

appear to offer the most significant source of hope for paleontologists seeking to uncover clues about the maritime journey. It is on the small north pacific islands where a few specialized paleontologists have focused on locating ancient fossils. When these scientists started their work, the initial goal was to deepen the knowledge of the history of the local Indigenous Peoples of the area. They developed new techniques and skills to recover marine and coastal artifacts.

Over the past few years, as more information confirms the validity of the Kelp Highway Theory, it became clear that the best place to look for artifacts from the Indigenous People's migration is on the islands in the North Pacific. Although, as previously mentioned, because the water level has risen, the geography of the Pacific coastline is quite different now than it was over 20,000 years ago when those brave first humans traveled the icy Pacific to the

Americas.

However, paleoecologists have discovered another fascinating factor: The land on the pacific coastline rose, just as a flattened sponge would, once the weight of the nearly two-mile tall glaciers was released. This effect was good news for paleontologists and archaeologists, as it seems that the coastline in that area, unlike some other places, is not so far from what it was when the Indigenous People were making their way to present-day America.

Scientists are also fortunate to have access to the very complex and sophisticated technology that enables them to use aerial imaging to calculate the coastline from 20,000 years ago. This technology helps them identify which islands or coastal areas are more likely to have significant archaeological sites. This technology can streamline the process of site selection and has led to the discovery of hundreds of artifacts that continue to support the possibility of the maritime migration theory.

CHAPTER 3

THE STORY OF THE INDIGENOUS PEOPLE IN THE AMERICAS

Indigenous knowledge has always been passed on verbally from one generation to the next. The Canadian History Museum describes the importance of the Indigenous tradition of oral history sharing in this way:

> First Peoples remember their origins through oral histories passed down by

elders in each generation.

These narratives describe the creation of the world and how the First Peoples came to live in it. More than legends, they embody a view of how the world fits together, and how human beings should behave in it.

Some oral histories refer to a time before human occupation. Others mark significant geographical, spiritual, and life events that have occurred over the millennia. (n.d. para 1-3)

The stories are sacred, and great attention is given to maintaining the authentic tradition of sharing history in this way. It must be understood and respected that this particular way of recording history is central to Indigenous culture and ways of knowing.

Indigenous Ways of Knowing

Before moving into the various origin stories of the Indigenous Peoples of North America, it is essential to understand that Indigenous ways of knowing are distinct from the concepts of Western knowledge. Unlike the Western view that knowledge must be tested and 'proven' to be validated, Indigenous ways of knowing to encompass a broader affirmation and validity of knowledge from many sources. For this reason, many Indigenous people don't believe in or support the need for scientific evidence to show how the People came to live in North America. It may be hurtful and controversial for many Indigenous People and communities to have Western scientists excavating the land and removing ancestral remains.

So far, the information in this book has been

exclusively rooted in Western views of knowledge, including the Western need to 'discover' and 'prove' how the Indigenous Peoples arrived in North America. A perspective more grounded in Indigenous ways of knowing would recognize that each nation has an origin story passed down since the Indigenous People arrived in North America.

In some Indigenous cultures, North America is called Turtle Island. These origin stories, recorded and transmitted orally, are the true and valid history of how each nation came to live on Turtle Island. It must also be noted that there are many Indigenous Nations on Turtle Island with many distinct histories and unique cultural characteristics. There does not exist one Indigenous history or one specific Indigenous way of knowing; each Indigenous nation is different from another to varying degrees. Some Indigenous Nations may appear to have overlapping values and cultures, others may not.

Characteristics of Indigenous ways of knowing that are central to many Indigenous Nation cultures include holistic views of the world in which we live. A holistic view considers the many relationships that exist between an individual and their family, their community, their environment, the food they eat, the places they go, and how they might interact with those places. Many Indigenous cultures emphasize a natural awareness and consider not just an individual but the individual *in relation* to others and the land. Generally, the effects of one's actions upon others and the land are more recognized and valued in Indigenous cultures than Western cultures. We can also describe that worldview as *relational*.

In Western cultures, values and actions often revolve around the idea of capitalism so that each person should try to get as much as possible for themselves, regardless of the outcome it might have on other people or the land and environment. It is generally considered valid, understandable, and even admirable for an individual in Western culture to hoard wealth and resources away from others.

The radically opposing fundamental worldviews, values, and ways of knowing between Indigenous Peoples and the Western European colonizers led to catastrophic outcomes for Indigenous People on Turtle Island. Indigenous Peoples had not encountered the capitalist mindset before colonialism. Having no understanding that such ways of being were even possible, they were taken advantage of in that regard.

Themes of Indigenous Creation Stories

Storytelling, especially the sharing of creation stories, is a cornerstone of nearly all Indigenous cultures. It is how information and wisdom pass from one generation to the next. Storytellers are deeply respected and honored in most Indigenous communities as they maintain and share knowledge and history. It can't be overemphasized how much the practice of this oral history tradition means to Indigenous culture and ways of knowing. It should be regarded as sacred and an equally valid way of learning and sharing information.

For the most part, each Indigenous nation has its own creation story, describing how humans came to exist. Many creation stories also explain how the land and animals came into existence, but in many others, the land was already there when humans were.

Although each Nation has its own creation story, there are common themes in many of them. Animals tend to feature heavily in many creation stories. In some stories, an animal is the creator of humans. For example, in the Salinan creation story, the bald eagle is the creator of the humans and makes them first out of clay. Certain animals are common, showing up as a creator or central character in several creation stories. For example, the crow, bald eagle, coyote, horse, and bear appear in many creation stories.

Another common theme in Indigenous creation stories is the need to find a balance, or how the People found peace. In nearly all the creation stories, humans come to land after the animals. In some creation stories, once humans were created, they disrupted a natural balance of what came before them. In other stories, they were out of balance in their attitudes and actions and learning through experience that greed and conflict are not helpful. In their process of experiential growth, humans learned that working cooperatively with each other and with the animals and environment is the most harmonious and peaceful way of being.

Natural disasters are also a common element in some creation stories. It seems that most of the time when natural disasters are a part of creation stories, it is to learn to respect the elements and nature or to overcome a time of turmoil to find peace through cooperation. Many Indigenous stories (other than creation stories) were also used to document and recount severe natural disasters. It often seems these disasters are floods, and there is a deep respect for water as it is viewed as the lifeblood of Mother Earth; it is revered for being so powerful.

Anishinaabe Creation Story

Here is an Anishinaabe Peoples' Creation story. It is a beautiful example of the types of themes are seen in many Indigenous creation stories including the Creator, or Great Spirit called 'Gitchi Manitou', the personification of Earth as a mother being, the use of the four directions to represent different parts that make up a whole, the mention of the importance and power of water, and the union of 'man' with Earth and with the animals.

When the Earth was young, it had a family. The Moon is called Grandmother, and the Sun is called Grandfather. This family is the basis of all creation in the universe. This family was created by Gitchi Manitou, the Creator. Earth is said to be a woman. She preceded man and her name is Mother Earth because all living things live from her gifts. Water is her lifeblood. It flows through her, nourishes her, and purifies her.

Mother Earth was given Four Sacred Directions – North, South, East, and West. Each direction contributes a vital part of her wholeness. Each direction and all things on Mother Earth have physical powers and spiritual powers.

When she was young, Mother Earth was filled with beauty. The Creator sent his singers in the form of birds to carry the seeds of life to all of the Four Sacred Directions. Life was spread across the land. The Creator placed the swimming creatures in the water. He placed the crawling things and the four-legged animals on the land. He gave life to all the plants and insects of the world. All parts of life lived in harmony with each other on Mother Earth.

Gitchi Manitou took the four parts of Mother Earth and blew them into a Sacred Megis Shell. From the union of the Four Sacred Elements and his breath, a man was created. It is said that Gitchi Manitou then lowered the man to the Earth. Thus, the man was the last form of life to be placed on Earth. From this Original Man came the Anishinaabe people. This man was created in the image of Gitchi Manitou. Man was part of Mother Earth. He lived in a brotherhood with all life that surrounded him. (Parks Canada Agency, 2018, para 1-4)

CHAPTER 4

THE INDIGENOUS RELATIONSHIP WITH THE LAND

Indigenous cultures, although each unique, hold a completely different view of land use and the human relationship with the land than western colonists. Pre-colonization, the concept of ownership never existed in Indigenous cultures. Before the Europeans arrived in the Americas, the land was not divided into states. In pre-contact America, there were no borders or precise measurements of land, which was far different from how it is today. For this reason, many Indigenous people and some non-Indigenous people do not recognize or use the colonial names for places.

The Indigenous views of land use and relationship are very different from how the European settlers viewed land ownership and usage; and very different from how the western colonial descendants continue to view it. Up until roughly 500 years ago, Indigenous nations occupied large territories and sustainably lived off the land. The cultures and lifestyles of each nation were shaped by the environment and geography of the land they occupied. The traditional Indigenous way of life was a delicate and complex relationship between the land and the people that was symbiotic and inextricable.

Indigenous Peoples of the pre-contact era did

not conceptualize land ownership, currencies such as money, and certainly not land as "real-estate." The Indigenous view of the land is one of resources and stewardship, of living off as well as with the land in a natural way. The Indigenous Peoples recognized that Mother Earth supplied them with all that was needed to live well. They also realized that it was necessary to steward and foster Mother Earth's ability to provide. Indigenous people commonly knew that nature and the resources from it must be respected and used only as needed and in moderation; otherwise, Mother Earth may not be able to continue to provide it. This profound wisdom was how Indigenous Nations were able to live sustainably since time immemorial. Because the tradition was to take only as much as was needed and value what was being used as a life-giving offering, the Indigenous Peoples didn't need to change their lifestyle or seek more resources. They were able to responsibly manage the land and their use of resources to live comfortably.

The traditional Indigenous way of life was utterly unknown and uninterpretable to the European settlers' view of Earth and natural resources. Europeans had a long history of property and resource ownership. Before Europeans landed in the Americas, they already had a long history of profiting off basic human necessities. In their culture, it was considered morally correct to hoard food and shelter and then to let people die because they could not access those basic necessities, even though the necessities did exist plentifully. As a result of the European beliefs that land and resources were commodities, combined with their seemingly insatiable desire to consume and hoard more resources, Europeans were forced to continually seek out additional resources via colonialism. Sadly, as a result of colonialism, many common so-called European moral beliefs, such as the use of land and resources as commodities, have increased across the globe.

Indigenous Territories

It's hard to clearly describe the traditional territories of the Indigenous Nations in the Americas because they were not necessarily clearly defined boundaries as we are accustomed to seeing today. The territories of many Nations are somewhat complex as many of the boundaries were porous, and the territories were overlapping. Some Indigenous Nations worked together in close relationships, while others had more firm boundaries between them.

Here is a non-exhaustive list of the traditional territories.

The far north of North America is the traditional territory of many Indigenous Nations. Given the ability to live in balance with some of the harshest conditions on the planet, it is safe to say that these are some of the strongest and most robust people in the world. From west to east, the nations that occupy this land are Inupiat, Kuskokwim, Eyak, Tlingit, Koyukon, Teslin Tlingit, Dene, Beaver, Tanana, Got'ine, Dënéndeh, Métis, Gwich'in Nành, Inuvialuit, Inuit, Naskapi, Inughuit Nunaat, and Kalaallit Nunaat.

Still in the north of the continent but descending into the more densely populated parallels, where seasons are distinct, yet more forgiving than in the far north, are the territories of Haida, Coast Salish, Okanagan, Syilx, Wet'suwet'en, Dënédeh, Yekooche, Cree, Stoney, Métis, Plains Cree, Assiniboine, Anishinabewaki, Wabanaki, Mi'kmaq'i, and the former Beothuk people. In this region of the continent, average temperatures are warmer, and growing seasons are longer. At this level of the globe, there is a drastic change in the climates as we move from the wet and temperate west coast, through the rugged mountains, across the extremes of the prairies, into densely forested woodland, and back out to coastal conditions on the east side of the continent. The diversity of the environments of the territories is reflected in the diversity of the Indigenous Nations that occupy them.

Moving down toward the present-day border between the United States and Canada are the territories of these Indigenous Nations: Quatsino, Squamish, Salish, Makah, Nisquali, Smish, K'ómoks, Yakama, Spokane, Chelan, Cheyenne, Niitsítapi (Blackfoot), Anishinabewaki, Mississauga, and Kanien'kehá:ka (Mohawk).

From west to east at the mid-latitudes in the United States are the traditional lands of Kalapuya, Siletz, Lakota, Dakota, Chinook, Pomo, Yuki, Yahooskin, Numu, Newe, Nimiipuu

(Nez Perce), Shoshone-Bannock, Eastern Shoshone, and Cheyenne.

In the Southern United States, roughly from west to east are the territories Confederation of the Siletz Indians, Numu, Newe, Shoshone-Bannock, Pueblos, Comanche, Apache, Peoria, Osage, Shawnee, Tsalaguwetiyi, Creek, Choctaw, and Lumbee.

In present-day Mexico, we find the traditional territory of these Indigenous Nations and civilizations: Cocohimí, Guaycura, Jojocobas, Tepehuán, Coahuiltecan, Gwachichi, Mexihcah, Nahua, Zapoteco, Aztec, Maya, Chorotega, and Rama.

CHAPTER 5
TRADITIONAL LIFESTYLES AND CULTURES

The geographic location and environment that each Indigenous Nation historically occupied shaped the lifestyle and resulting culture. Although all Indigenous Nations are distinct, there do tend to be more overlapping similarities between cultures of Indigenous Nations that evolved to survive in similar environments. Geographically close groups tend to share cultural similarities because a sizable part of traditional Indigenous lifestyles revolved around procuring the necessities for survival, such as hunting and gathering practices, clothing fabrication techniques, types of tools, and housing.

There are also far too many individual nations to list all of them and their unique lifestyles. For this reason, traditional Indigenous lifestyles are best described by region rather than by specific nation or group. In the case of an Indigenous nation whose lifestyle and culture was quite different from the regional norms of the area surrounding their territory.

The Inuit Nations of the Far North

Most Indigenous peoples in the far north are Inuit (Inuvialuit) or related to the Inuit culture. Inuit have lived in the Arctic for over 4,000 years and adapted specialized skills for surviving there.

Being efficient is probably more important in the harsh conditions of the Arctic than anywhere else in the world. Each season in the far north is distinct and must be used in its own way to maximize productivity. Because many foods or items were only available seasonally, the Inuk spent much of the year preparing for the long, intense winters; that preparation was key to survival.

The traditional lifestyle of the Inuit was semi-nomadic. The community groups migrated a few times a year with the change of the seasons. Each community group traveled to the same specific and known sites year after year to hunt, gather, fish, or harvest other necessary items.

The times for migration would vary from one

year to the next, depending on the weather and the animals; this is one example of the ways and reasons that most Indigenous Nations are so intertwined with nature. The traditional way of the Inuit was to take the cue from the environment and act in response to that, moving in step with the natural world.

Traditionally, caribou were a substantial part of the Inuit subsistence and would influence migration for the hunting pods twice a year. The massive caribou herd would migrate north in the spring and south in the fall. During those times of the year, when the caribou were gathered in such large numbers, it was easier for the Inuks to hunt them successfully. It was important for the Inuit groups to have their camps established in strategic locations to make hunting and processing the caribou most efficient in the spring and fall. The fall caribou hunting season was crucial as it provided a large portion of the food and fur that the Inuit groups would need to use for survival throughout the winter. If something went wrong during the fall hunt, it might mean a lack of food for winter, and the result of that could potentially be deadly.

Spring and fall camps consisted of tent-like shelter structures made from small logs as posts and animal skins as the sides and roof. These structures could be transported and reassembled relatively quickly, making them ideal for the needs of the Inuit groups as they migrated with changing seasons.

In the winter months, Inuks traditionally built shelters out of ice blocks. Because of the size and design of the ice shelters, they could even have fires inside the ice homes, called igloos. The igloo walls were many inches thick and provided a solid protective structure that was well insulated all winter long.

The Inuit hunted seals for meat and fur during the winter months. It was customary for all Indigenous Nations to use all parts of the animals they hunted. The meat for eating, the skin for clothing, and the bones for tools or jewelry. Nothing was wasted, and animals were not hunted unless needed and entirely used.

For travel in the winter months and to transport items over snow, Inuks designed and crafted sleds. They used bones or branches with animal hides to build multi-functional sleds that were light and durable. The Inuit would also use domesticated dogs to help pull the sleds.

Winter is very long and very dark in the Arctic region. Inuks spent a lot of time during winter in igloos with their family. Traditionally winter was when stories, craftwork, games, songs, and dances were passed on to younger generations;

and practiced for fun to keep occupied over the many months of winter.

When the days got longer and the snow began to melt, the Inuit knew it was time to start to prepare for the spring. For each hunting group, this meant migrating to their specific spring camp location in hopes of harvesting as many caribou as needed while the massive herds migrate north for the summer. After a long winter of living off mainly seal meat, spring was likely an exciting time to begin to diversify the diet once again, starting with the caribou, then with fresh plants and berries as they become available throughout the summer.

For the most part, Inuit lived near the ocean year-round, although in the Arctic, for much of the year, the ice was so thick, you would hardly be able to tell there was ocean beneath it or nearby. They relied heavily on what the sea provided for food and ate primarily meat and fish year-round.

Traditionally, many of the Inuit family hunting groups camped near an accessible coast in the summer months. They designed and used kayaks to travel long distances over water very efficiently. Inuks were master anglers, hunting and catching all types of edible and valuable marine animals, even as large as whales.

Inuit clothing was made from animal furs and hides. Seemingly miraculously, but as in all other aspects of life, Mother Earth provided the People with all that was necessary for survival in the Arctic climate. The furs of the animals they hunted for food were exactly what was needed to protect them against the harsh elements of the far north. Seal fur made a perfectly warm and waterproof material that Inuks traditionally used for mittens, boots, coats, baby wraps, and more.

The people themselves tended to be of small stature and naturally very fit and strong due to lifestyle. Their bodies would adapt and change with the seasons, as they were more active in certain months and had more food to live off in those months as well. Just like everything else in the natural environment, they themselves changed naturally over the course of the year. The Inuk's facial features, hair, and skin resemble the typical features of many Asiatic-related groups.

The traditional Inuit culture was very communal and interconnected. Most of the community groups consisted of family pods that included a mother, father, children, often an adopted child or niece or nephew, and relatives such as siblings who were not married, and sometimes the grandparents as well, especially as they aged. A few related family pods would often group together in a commune to share work and life.

Inuit always worked together to accomplish tasks and keep the community fed, clothed, and housed; they shared the labor and the fruits unilaterally. Even though everyone had unique strengths or talents, each individual offered their abilities to serve the group and shared equally in the resources and outcomes. Working together in that way was essential to survival in the harsh conditions of the territory they occupied; no one could survive in the Arctic on their own. At some point, everyone in the group would need to receive and offer help.

The Inuit created a deep connection to nature by being in tune with environmental changes in their natural habitat and living organically in response. Traditionally, the Inuit viewed themselves as one with Mother Earth, not as humans separate from it. This connection with the Earth is a fundamental and distinguishing feature of traditional Indigenous culture that differs drastically from European settler worldviews. The colonizers lacked an understanding of the relationship between the Indigenous Nations and the land. This lack of knowledge led colonizers to make poor and arrogant choices regarding the treatment of the humans and the land they encountered in the Americas, decisions which have led to the extinction of countless species of plants and animals, and even ultimately to climate change.

Post-Colonial Contact in the Arctic

At the time of contact in the 1500s, on the East Coast of North America, Indigenous Peoples were living almost exactly the way they had been for, in some cases, over 10 thousand years. European contact changed that completely. The specific effects of contact and colonialism were different for Nations in other parts of the continent. However, over time the European settlers completely altered the Indigenous way of life to the point that it no longer functioned for survival, let alone in the beautiful symbiotic and sustainable way of life that it had provided for time immemorial.

Inuit contact with Europeans started in the east, as Europeans arrived from that direction and then progressed westward over the course of 100-150 years. The first Inuit to encounter the Europeans lived in Labrador and encountered explorers first. After the explorers, Inuit contact with settlers slowly increased over time as European settlers sailed north seasonally to hunt whales; the whalers would interact with or trade with Indigenous communities when they did. At first, the contact was relatively minimal and did not significantly alter the Inuit's way of life; they continued to move seasonally and maximize the use of natural resources available in each season.

Over time some Inuks began to travel south in the summer to trade in the settler villages, they exchanged furs for metal tools, blankets, clothing, and other valuable items. It was trading with settlers that slowly altered the way of life for Inuks by introducing new technologies. Although this type of trade seemed unintrusive at first, it was the beginning of the change from exclusively Indigenous ways of living to an ultimately unsustainable European-influenced lifestyle. It also introduced Indigenous Peoples to the European system of values, a capitalist system based on currency, private property ownership, and greed which was utterly different from the Inuit values.

As contact between the two cultures continued

to increase, disputes and conflicts between the Inuit and the settlers became more frequent. It was in the 1700s, when more demand for whale fat increased the whaling activity and contact in the Far North, with whalers becoming commonplace in the North over the summer months. Eventually, in the 1800s, whaling activity became year-round in the Arctic, and Inuit communities were continuously in contact with European Settlers.

One of the first detrimental effects of increased contact was the transmission of diseases from the settlers to the Inuit. The Indigenous Peoples in the Americas all suffered greatly as the new illnesses swept through communities killing many.

Another detrimental effect of contact and settlement that impacted the Inuit culture and lifestyle was the over-harvesting of marine animals, such as whales. Although Inuit had lived in the Arctic for time immemorial and had harvested all types of marine animals, including whales, for thousands of years, they had always practiced sustainable and responsible hunting and harvesting techniques. The new settlers and whalers from Europe quickly overharvested the whale population within a matter of several decades. Overharvesting altered the relationship of the Inuit with the land and animals that they had relied upon for generations. As the supply and demand for whale fat diminished, the fur trade experienced an uptick in demand, which brought even more settlers to the arctic searching for pelts for the European fashion industry.

During that time, tensions mounted as culture clashes and misunderstandings led to increasing conflicts between the Inuits and the settlers. Colonizers began to feel the need to assimilate Inuit to the European settlers' culture and lifestyle. They believed it would relieve tensions between the cultures if they could eliminate the traditional cultures and alter the Inuit's way of life to better suit the needs of the growing settler population. Missions were established throughout the North starting in the mid to late 1700s. The missions were used as a school structure to teach Inuit how to read and write in Inuktitut and English. The missionaries also taught the Inuks Christianity with the goal of teaching the Inuks to adopt the new European way of life and leave the traditional Inuit culture behind. In some cases, in hopes of minimizing contact and easing tensions between the raiders and the Indigenous Peoples, the missionaries also took over the trade interactions between the European fur traders and the Indigenous hunters.

Over the course of the 200 years that followed contact, most Inuit were converted to Christianity. The shift to Christianity changed the fundamental views that shaped the culture and lifestyle of the Inuit. Although many may view it as a negative shift and part of colonialism, many Inuit are Christian to this day.

As time went on, settlers used more resources in unsustainable ways and started establishing villages further north. Many Inuit communities were relocated to more northern villages by the government, this forced them to adapt their traditional way of life to territories that were not natural for them to inhabit in the new way that was expected of them; of course, that didn't work.

No one was aware of how delicate the balance of Indigenous life was in the Arctic, nor did they appreciate that it had been finely tuned over the course of millennia. The effects of the loss of culture and lifestyle were more harmful to the outcomes of the Inuit than anyone would have guessed. The loss of culture and lifestyle was extremely traumatic for the Inuit, without the traditional methods of hunting and survival many foods and resources became scarce and many lived in poverty conditions. To further add to the trauma of this upheaval was the utterly traumatic effects of the "residential schools" which will be discussed in a chapter all on its own.

The Haida People of the Pacific Northwest

Traditionally, many distinct Nations occupied the Pacific Coast on the mainland and on the many small islands around it. Despite having different cultures and languages, these Indigenous Nations shared at least one powerful resource in common: the ocean. The ocean defined the way of life for the traditional occupants of these beautiful territories. The

People of the coast were well adapted to traveling over water and harvesting the abundant marine life that the Pacific Ocean had to offer.

The climate along the coast was drastically milder than the far north or even than other inland territories at the same latitudes. The Indigenous Peoples along the coast benefited from more forgiving temperatures and weather. They also benefited from the long growing season with ample diversity of flora and fauna in their territories. Finding food for survival was rarely an issue for the Indigenous Peoples of the Pacific Northwest.

The Haida Tribe

The Haida People lived on The Haida Gwaii archipelago, a grouping of islands off the northwest coast of present-day British Columbia. There is evidence that the Haida have occupied that area for over 19,000 years. The entire area is thought to have been inhabitable even during the Ice Age-era as it would have been the southeastern part of Beringia. Based on traditional stories of the People living alongside the glaciers and western scientific methods, it is believed that the Haida people lived in the same territory during the Ice Age. When the Haida would have made their home in that area, the sea level was much lower, and the water that now separates the islands from the mainland would have been shallow and easily passable on foot throughout most of the year. The Haida had occupied their territory since a time when the rest of the world was covered with unfathomably massive glaciers.

After the Ice Age, the landscape began to change as the water levels gradually rose. The Haida people naturally adapted to a mariner lifestyle. They used the giant red cedars in their territory for many purposes, including dugout canoes of various sizes and uses. The Haida could travel quickly from island to island or the mainland with the canoes.

Food sources were plentiful on the Pacific Coast and offered the Haida People a diverse and nutritious diet. Their traditional diet included many fish and marine animals such as seals and whales. The Haida territory was also fortunate to have beavers, deer, bears, wolves, foxes, elk, and moose in their native environment. The people hunted whenever possible for food, pelts, and other parts. Unlike their Inuk neighbors in the north, the Haida and other coastal peoples also had access to abundant plants throughout the seasons, including fresh leafy greens and delicious berries.

The Haida had a unique culture, including a seemingly complex social structure based on hierarchy groupings, including enslaving people from conflicts with mainland tribes; other tribes knew them to be warriors, with a culture not unlike the Vikings.

The social structure of the Haida people was composed of two caste-like groups or *moieties*. The moieties were called the Raven Clan and the Eagle Clan. Each group held access to clan territories for hunting, fishing, or other resources that only clan members had the right to use. The moieties were made up of several closely related family group households of 30 or more people. Traditionally, the Haida was a matrilineal-based society, so the mother's relations determine the clan membership. There were many family groups in each clan, and every family had a male hereditary chief. Still, his heredity of the chiefdom was determined through matrilineal descent. The passing chief's eldest sister's son would be in line to be chief. Each household lived in their own large home with allotted land but alongside the other families of the same moiety.

Each clan was distinct and had its own traditional stories, songs, dances, and carving designs that the elders taught to the younger generations. Each generation took great pride in learning and maintaining the knowledge, cultural practices, and history.

Traditionally, when marriages took place, they were strictly between members of opposite clans to maintain diplomacy and diversity. The group that a child was a part of was determined matrilineally, meaning that they were members of the same group that their mothers were from, either Eagle or Raven.

In the traditional Haida culture, chores and duties were divided into gender roles for the most part. The Haida men were responsible for hunting, fishing, crafting canoes, homes, totems, and war-related activities. In the Haida culture, women were responsible for maintaining the living space—inside and out—and foraging for fruits and plants, caring for children, making clothing, and preparing food.

The unique and intricate traditional Haida culture is renowned for many things, but perhaps most notably for their artwork and craftsman skills. The Haida men were known as expert carvers, a skill that continues to be passed down today. They were known for carving giant canoes out of a single red cedar trunk. Some of the canoes were so large they could hold 50 people. The canoes were decorated with ornate carvings of animals that represented spirits and myths.

The Haida are perhaps most well-known for carving totem poles from giant red cedars. Other

Indigenous Nations along the Pacific Coast also carved totem poles. The totems could range in size depending on the tree it was carved from; some were up to 70 feet in height. The style of the carvings on the totems was unique to the Haida and to the other coastal Indigenous Peoples who carved them. Totem poles were carved for many reasons, including to signify clan membership or show family lineage and honor certain myths, animals, people or events.

For most of the post-colonial era, European settlers believed that Indigenous culture was inherently evil and actively tried to eliminate it. From the late 1800s until the first few decades of the 1900s, European settlers banned, removed, and destroyed totems and other culturally significant Indigenous crafts and ceremonies. However, totems are now a famous and iconic symbol of Indigenous art and culture. Many people of all backgrounds travel to Haida Gwaii and other west coast destinations to view some of the oldest and tallest totem poles that remain in their original locations.

The large houses that the Haida families lived in were also built from the same red cedar as the canoes and totem poles, which were plentiful in the territory. The homes were large square-shaped structures that were windowless, though they did have venting in the ceiling to release the smoke from the fires that were used for heating and cooking. Each of the large buildings was home to one household of 30 or more people, including several nuclear families that were now-grown siblings who had spouses and children, other non-married family members, and elders. As previously mentioned, each of these households had a hereditary chief and preserved their history through stories, myths, songs, and carvings.

One of the main ceremonies that Haida

practiced was the Potlatch ceremony. Potlatches were held for many reasons including to honor a passing or a birth. The ceremonies also served as a social event and could even be political in nature. Potlatches were used to demonstrate to others how wealthy and powerful a family was; all the hosts' valuable possessions including even enslaved laborers would be on display to prove their status in the community. The chief of the family hosting the Potlatch would offer gifts to all who came, including art, tools, boats, food, enslaved laborers, or territory rights for hunting and fishing. The ceremonies included ornate costumes, songs, and dance. The guests would be expected to remember and recount this generosity and wealth to continue to build up the host family's reputation of high social status and history. Negotiations between households or tribes could take place at Potlatches as well.

Haida spirituality was rooted in animal spirits

and mythology based on Trickster spirits. They believed that animals were special, magical humans that could shape change into an animal or a human. It was believed that through reincarnation people's souls lived on in other physical forms, including animals. Each household had its own stories and beliefs about who had been reincarnated and on what farm, as well as stories about special animals that had been encountered.

A central figure of traditional Haida spirituality and mythology was the Raven Trickster. As a trickster spirit, the Raven was said to have the ability to go between the spiritual plane and the physical world. Raven was not considered to be a God but was the most powerful spirit in the Haida culture and spiritual beliefs. Raven was known as a benevolent trickster who enjoyed playfully confusing humans but did not cause harm unless provoked maliciously in some way.

There are many stories about Raven, called Wee'git in the Haida language, causing mischief and showing examples of why not to break rules, or playfully discovering misadventures because of his curiosity. There are many metaphors and themes that the Wee'git stories teach, including lightheartedness and curiosity.

In the Haida creation story, Wee'git uncovered the first Haida in a clamshell, here is a telling of the Haida Creation Story:

> According to Haida legend, the Raven found himself alone one day on Rose Spit beach, on Haida Gwaii. Suddenly, he saw an extraordinary clamshell at his feet, and protruding from it were a number of small creatures. The Raven coaxed them to leave the shell to join him in his wonderful world. Some were hesitant at

first, but eventually, overcome by curiosity, they emerged from the partly open clamshell to become the first Haida. (Raven Reads, 2018, para 12)

The Haida were proud warrior people with no fear of conflict or war. Traditionally the Haida warriors traveled by sea in huge carved cedar canoes which could hold up to 60 warriors. They traveled by sea to destinations both near and far, with stories recounting exploration and travel as far as California and Asia.

The warriors would paddle along the coast to trade with neighboring communities or simply to raid their adversaries' villages. During raids, the Haida would gain hunting or fishing territory, copper, and other precious resources. It symbolized power and prominence in Haida society to have many resources and keep enslaved laborers, whom the warriors acquired through raiding.

Traditional Haida warriors wore distinctive helmets ornately carved from cedar as well. For weapons, they used bows and arrows, spears, blowguns, clubs, daggers, and later firearms that they could carry in the canoes with them. They had shields to defend themselves from arrows and attacks as they approached the villages by the sea.

The Haida were formidable military strategists and expertly fortified their Island territory with towers, look-outs, and traps. Due to the geography of their homeland and their keen defense systems, they were virtually untouchable. From the towers, they could monitor the sea and beaches for any unwanted approaching boats and form an attack on them before they even landed on the shore. When European explorers began making contact along the west coast, they often documented the impressive and intimidating Haida warriors.

The Haida and Colonization

It wasn't until the 1770s that Europeans made their way to the pacific northwest and into the Haida territory. By all European accounts from the time of contact, they were impressed by the Haida Nation. The Europeans document an admiration for the Haida's defense system and the military's formidable seafaring abilities.

At the time of Haida's contact with the European explorers, the Haida had never seen or heard of non-Indigenous people. In contrast, the explorers had already encountered and probably interacted with a fair number of Indigenous Peoples on their travels. This left the Haida at a disadvantage. They mistook the pale European explorers as spirit people with different means and technology from their own.

The Haida welcomed the newcomers because they believed that they were ancestral spirits of some kind.

At that time, the fur trade was a significant economic driver for the Europeans, and they soon began trading goods with the Haida in exchange for furs, which then were traded to merchants in China. As contact and trade increased relatively quickly on the west coast, compared to the east, the Haida soon replaced their traditional weapons for firearms that they traded for pelts.

As was the fate of all Indigenous Nations post-contact, the Haida contracted many illnesses from the European traders, including deadly smallpox and tuberculosis. It is estimated that these diseases were responsible for killing 95% of the Haida population; from such a great loss, the Nation never recovered. Today census data confirms that 501 people identify themselves as being of Haida descent, with 445 people still being able to speak the Haida language (Dorothy-Kennedy & Bouchard, 2010).

Despite a peaceful beginning to the relationship between the Haida and the European traders, tensions eventually mounted as more permanent European settlements were established in the area surrounding Haida Gwaii. The settlers and their emerging government believed that Indigenous traditions and customs were evil and the root cause of conflict between the two cultures. During the late 1800s, the settlers started to assert dominance and control over the Haida people and all Indigenous Nations in the pacific northwest. They enacted laws to eliminate Indigenous culture by banning traditional practices such as Potlatches and Totem Poles.

Throughout the 1900s, as the Haida population, culture, and traditional way of life had significantly declined, the settler government continued the campaign to further assimilate Indigenous Peoples by forcing Indigenous children from all parts of the continent into what are euphemistically called "residential schools." Today, most people referring to this practice refuse to call the institutions *schools* because they functioned more like forced detention facilities for children and youth; for that reason, in this book, that term is within quotations.

The outcomes of "residential schools" were devastating for the Haida, as it was for all Indigenous peoples. Children were forcibly and traumatically removed from their families and relocated to the "residential schools." The trauma affected parents and children alike and led to a disruption in appropriate cultural and family-based learning. Essential aspects of parental attachment were lost, not to mention that parenting skills are actually learned through modeling in a family setting; the disruption of that process resulted in a lack of continuity of socio-generational learning in a family environment; essentially, most Indigenous children during that era were not given the opportunity to be loved and parented, nor were they then able to learn how to be a parent.

The practice of removing children from their families went on for several generations. The trauma and effects were compounded with each generation until all that remained was a frail shell of a formerly glorious Nation. The language, culture, and joy were all but extinguished through these horrific colonial practices.

"Residential schools" have not been in operation

for the past few decades, and though most of them closed before then, the effects remain today. In fact, very recently, thousands of stolen Indigenous children's remains have been discovered on the grounds of many former "residential schools." It is expected that as more former "residential school" sites are excavated that more missing children's remains will be uncovered. For Indigenous people, these findings are retraumatizing, but the discovery of the missing children's remains does allow for them to be returned to their families and communities. There is hope that this can at least bring some sense of closure and that a healing process may begin. It may also be true that the discovery of the gravesites brings further awareness to the true cruelty that took place in "residential schools"; a truth that was always known by Indigenous survivors and families, but that had been diminished or denied by governments over the past century.

The Nehiyawak (Cree) Nation in the Plains

Cree is the Anglicized name of the Nehiyawak Peoples, dubbed *Cree* due to miscommunication early on in their relationship with European trappers and settlers in the northeast. Traditionally the Nehiyawak Peoples' territory stretched across nearly the entire span of present-day Canada, from east of the Great Lakes, across the plains, to the foothills of the Rocky Mountains. The traditional lifestyle of the Nehiyawak was completely nomadic and involved following game across the great northern plains and sub-arctic boreal forests of the continent, which is why the Traditional Nehiyawak territory is so vast.

The Nehiyawak lived in relatively small family groups called a lodge. The members of each lodge would share daily living and labor tasks and would usually reside together in one tipi. Many lodges are grouped to form a community called a band. The band would collectively migrate to meet the seasonal needs together for most of the year.

Tipis were the main style of structure used by the nomadic Nehiyawak bands for shelter in all seasons. They are cone-shaped tents that the Nehiyawak people made from shaped wooden poles and buffalo, or sometimes other animal hides sewn together. There is evidence that Indigenous Peoples in the northern plains have been using tipis for over 5,000 years and even longer in the far north regions. This was the most common dwelling style for the Nehiyawak until the late 1800s when European settlers and government treaties forced Indigenous communities to stop living the traditional way and moved onto reservation land. Nowadays, tipis are generally only used for ceremonies and special events.

It was no coincidence that the tipi was the sheltering method of choice for nomadic bands since they were easy to erect and dismantle and relatively light to transport. Tipis were quite large; typically, they were anywhere between 12 and 20 feet wide at the base and stood 15 to 20 feet tall. Each tipi housed about 10 people, the average size of a lodge. An essential feature of the tipi was the hole in the very top point of the cone, which was necessary for venting the smoke from the fire that was used for cooking and heating.

For each season, the Nehiyawak had a different form of transportation to suit the climate and environment they would navigate. In the summer months, they would often use canoes to travel and transport their shelters swiftly and efficiently on water. Like everything that Indigenous Nations built and used, traditionally, canoes were made from what was available locally in their territories and for the needs of the people. Because of the different environmental requirements and readily available materials, the Nehiyawak and other inland Nations' canoes varied greatly from the Haida and west coast style canoes. The Nehiyawak made small, light canoes of birch bark; they created a spiny frame out of flexible branches and covered it with sewn birchbark flaps. These canoes were usually designed to hold only a few people with their gear and were more maneuverable than the large, heavy seafaring canoes that the Haida built.

In winter, the Nehiyawak people used sleds and snowshoes to traverse the deep snow. Like the canoes, sled frames were also made of birch wood. Animal hides were used to cover the frame and make a seat or platform for carrying gear. The sleds were different sizes depending on their use. Some sleds were pulled by dogs or horses while people simply pulled or pushed others. Traditionally, the Nehiyawak people used sleds to carry young children and belongings when migrating, or for hunting to carry supplies and to transport the animal.

Snowshoes are racquet-like woven platforms that were traditionally worn under moccasins and used to walk on top of the snow in winter, instead of sinking into the deep snow. They were traditionally made of birch wood and animal hide, bound tightly with a special rawhide weave to keep the structure.

The Nehiyawak used domesticated dogs and horses to help carry their belongings on a sled-like *travois*. A travois consisted of two birch wood poles joined together at a point on top to form a roughly triangular shape that was open at the bottom. Similar to a sled, objects of all sorts could be fastened to the travois and dragged along by the animal.

Traditional game hunted by the Nehiyawak would depend on the time of year and the territory that each group was familiar with or occupied. Often the Nehiyawak hunted and trapped large games such as deer, moose, elk, and caribou, and smaller games like rabbit, duck, turkey, and other birds or rodents that they could catch. Like all Indigenous peoples, the Nehiyawak lived sustainably; they hunted only as much as necessary and used every part of the animals they harvested.

Buffalo, which was plentiful in the prairies until 150 years ago, was a staple for the Paskwāwiyiniwak, the Plains Cree. The Paskwāwiyiniwak relied on the buffalo for food, hides, and trade with other bands and Nations. The giant animal could provide enough food for many people, and the thick hides had many traditional uses in the Nehiyawak culture. The Paskwāwiyiniwak used many techniques for hunting large animals, including bow and arrow, spears, and most efficiently, running them over a cliff's edge. In the plains, few locations worked as buffalo jump sites. Head-Smashed-In, located in southern Alberta (just north of the Canadian border from North Dakota), is a famous traditional site where the Paskwāwiyiniwak would run the buffalo over the cliffs. Buffalo bones collected at the cliff's foot were dated 6,000 years old. The Head-Smashed-In buffalo jump cliffs are a protected UNESCO World Heritage site to preserve the area and teach visitors to the park about Nehiyawak history.

Clothing was traditionally made by women in the Nehiyawak culture. Women would tan animal hides, especially deer, moose, and elk, to make leather for clothing and footwear. The women would then sew the clothing using needles made from animal bones and decorated with beadwork.

The Nehiyawak women mostly wore dresses made of leather with fringe and beadwork. The men wore coats with fringe cuts along the sleeves and decorative beadwork. The men's pants included underpants, similar to leggings or long johns, with leather chap-like panels called breechcloths over top. The pants were also decorated with beadwork and cut fringe. Typically, the clothing used in ceremonies and gatherings was more decorated with quills, furs, feathers, and ornate beadwork.

Moccasins are the handmade style of shoes that the Nehiyawak wore. Like the rest of the clothing, they were handmade by the women out of tanned hide and decorated the beadwork. Some moccasins were lined with fur on the inside to be extra warm or made into a taller boot style. Moccasins are still a popular and enduring Indigenous craft.

Intricate and ornate beading has been used in Indigenous peoples, including the Nehiyawak, to decorate clothing for at least 8,000 years. Each Nation, band, or even family has its own unique patterns and styles which are representative of the place, culture, and time the beader was working in. Traditionally beads were made of seeds, pieces of bones, small rocks, shells, and quills. The older styles of beading that have been discovered were larger and strung together like a necklace, rather than sewn directly onto the garment.

Traditional Nehiyawak Spirituality and Ceremonies

The most sacred ceremony in Nehiyawak culture was the Sun Dance. Each summer many bands of Indigenous Nations would gather for several days to dance and celebrate the gifts of life together. Depending on the size of the group gathered, they erected one or several lodges together to be used for the duration of the ceremony as shelter, kitchen, and for sweating. A sweat lodge was also constructed for the sweat ceremony that was held at the beginning of the Sun Dance.

The Sun Dance ceremony was an important cultural tradition for Indigenous Peoples of the great plains and surrounding areas. It was the main time for people from different bands or even nations to come together to share songs, dance, and mythology in a ceremonial way. The experience of collectivity and sharing on a large scale solidified the values and culture each year; it also wove a common social and cultural thread to all the bands and nations who came.

Traditionally, the Sun Dance would last several

days around the time of the summer solstice. This was a time to pray for healing and rebirth, sacrifices might be made for the good of the band or for an individual or family in need. The continuous dance and song of the ceremony were very intense for the dancers who would be dancing continuously in shifts for many days. This was the purpose of the ceremony, to sacrifice and continue the ceremony and practice despite the discomfort, to persevere and push past the personal obstacles as a sacred offering but also as an opportunity to discover one's own strength and capability. Some participants also performed other rituals based on the idea of creating a painful or challenging experience to overcome, for example, enduring skin piercing and pulling. The goal was to create a need to sacrifice personal comfort and to endure or overcome the sensation or physical needs that presented themselves through that experience.

The Sun Dance was also a time to check-in and learn from other bands and nations about things they had seen or heard over the years. Language and dialect varied between the bands and nations that came together during the Sun Dance. Generally, neighboring bands would have a more similar dialect than ones who lived further apart. Despite the dialect differences, Nehiyawak could understand each other, although sometimes it might have taken a bit of effort.

Bands could pass on the news to each other at the Sun Dance; for example, people could share information about the happenings in other parts of the vast territory such as floods or fires, births and passings, and so on. Or, as the European explorers and trappers appeared in some areas of the Nehiyawak territory, that was passed on through social networks, including at the Sun Dance and through the relationships developed there.

A sweat lodge ceremony was performed as a part of the Sun Dance gathering and, at other times as a distinct ceremony on its own. Sweat lodge ceremonies are still practiced by many of the Nehiyawak bands today. In the center of a sweat lodge is a fire pit, the participants of the sweat sit in a ring around the pit and depending on the size of the group may form several rings. Once all the guests are in the lodge, the fire tender brings in rocks and adds them to the pit in specific placements. At this point, the entrance was closed, and the ceremony began with prayer. Sometimes the host would guide a prayer or participants of the sweat would pray in whatever way was meaningful to them. At times, the fire tender would also pour water onto the rocks to create steam and increase the heat. The sweat could last for nearly 24 hours with breaks taken by participants to avoid dangerous overheating.

The vision quest is another integral aspect of Nehiyawak spirituality. Vision quests were primarily performed by boys or youth transitioning into adulthood. It took quite a bit of time and dedication for the youth and the elders to make sure that the vision quester was prepared and ready for the experience. For youth in the Nehiyawak culture, it was a rite of passage to complete a vision quest, it showed that he was mature and was able to survive on his own in the wild.

Vision quests taught youth many valuable skills, both practical, cultural, and spiritual. They learned about the value of working toward something and achieving the privilege and opportunity to partake in this sacred ceremony. The vision quest was a goal and a reason for them to put energy into learning essential survival skills and cultural knowledge.

During the vision quest, the participant would spend several days on his own in the wilderness. The quest combined a practical time for youth to use survival skills as well as for them to experience an altered state of awareness and spiritual awakening.

It was believed that in order to achieve this altered state of consciousness and enter the spiritual realm, the youth should endure survival on their own with limited food and sleep. This also brought the participant into deep communion with his own thoughts, feelings, and experiences. The outcomes and visions were different for everyone. The visions that came had a unique meaning for each person. The participant gained new spiritual knowledge and understanding that was completely personal. In many Indigenous cultures, the vision and experience were kept secret and private for the participant.

Tobacco was also considered a sacred medicine in many Indigenous cultures, it was used in several ceremonies, including the profoundly sacred pipe ceremony. It represents the connection between the earthly world and the spirit world. The plant itself has deep roots which grow in the earthly physical world, yet, once it is dried and burned, it becomes smoke, which moves it from the physical world into the spiritual realm. It is a powerful metaphor for all things that exist in the physical world and their impermanence and ability to be transformed into an ethereal matter that disperses into the spirit world.

Sharing the smoke from tobacco also connects the people and their spirits as it passes from one to the next, and into the body then out into the world to be dispersed and to circulate infinitely; in that way, the tobacco smoke is connecting and unifying. Sharing the smoke from tobacco in the ceremony represents the desire to connect and share peace among people and spirits.

Traditionally, the Nehiyawak used the sacred plant tobacco in many ways, including as medicine. As healing medicine, tobacco smoke was blown by a medicine man onto wounds or onto a person in need of healing. It was also used as an offering, for example, by laying tobacco in a field with a prayer for a good harvest. It could also be used for other types of prayers and offered to an elder, family member, spirits and ancestors, and the creator, Gitchi Manitou.

Gitchi Manitou is the Great Spirit, also known as the Creator of the world. 'Gitchi' means great and 'Manitou' means spirit, making Gitchi Manitou the Great Spirit. The Great Spirit is a formless and genderless entity, not associated with being human. It was Gitchi Manitou who created the Earth, the plants, animals, and the people.

In the story of creation, Gitchi Manitou first created the four sacred elements: rock, water, fire, and wind. From those elements, Gitchi Manitou then created the earth, sun, moon, and stars. After the physical world was made, Gitchi Manitou created four types of plants: trees, vegetables, grasses, and flowers. Next Gitchi Manitou created four types of animals: four-legged, two-legged, flying animals, and swimming animals. After everything else was created, Gitchi Manitou made humans. Humans were considered to be the weakest of all of the creatures but had the unique power to think and dream.

The sacred mythology of the Nehiyawak, like that of all Indigenous Peoples, centered around animal spirits. This reflected the deep connection to nature and animals that Indigenous Peoples had. Traditionally, they believed in reincarnation so that animals might have spirits of people and vice versa. The interconnectedness of the people with the animals and nature was also reflected in spirituality and the respect for the delicate balance of life. The Nehiyawak understood the consequences of when life got out of balance and did what was within their power to maintain the balance through the way of life and also through prayer and ceremony.

The Nehiyawak also believed in animal tricksters. Wisakedjak is a trickster spirit of great import to the Nehiyawak culture and heritage. There are countless stories about Wisakedjak, a friendly but mischievous character who broke rules and caused the natural order of things to be upset and altered. Each band or community would have their own Wisakedjak stories to tell and to pass onto the younger generation to be kept and passed on for generations to come. The Nehiyawak trickster stories varied between bands and across their vast territory.

Here is a Nehiyawak story of why Gitchi Manitou created the trickster Wisakedjak borrowed from explorer David Thompson:

> At the beginning of time, the Creator made the animals and the people. The Creator told Wisakedjak (a trickster figure) to teach the people how to live good, peaceful lives, and to take care of them. Wisakedjak did not listen to the Creator, and soon, the people were fighting and hurting one another. The Creator was disappointed and threatened Wisakedjak with a life of misery if he did not obey. Still, Wisakedjak did not listen, and still, the people continued to be

violent with one another. The Creator decided to flood the lands, washing out everyone and everything. Only Wisakedjak, Otter, Beaver, and Muskrat survived. Stranded on open water, Wisakedjak had an idea — if the animals could help him dive down and collect some of the old earth, he could expand it and start a new land. This was not an easy task; Otter and Beaver tried many times to get to the earth below, but both failed, almost dying in the process. Muskrat was the last to try. IIe stayed underwater for a long time, but when he resurfaced, he had wet earth in his paw. From this mud is where the earth as we know it today came. (Preston, 2018, Origin Story)

Spirituality was a big part of traditional Nehiyawak wellness and medicine. The Medicine Wheel represents the Nehiyawak views of medicine and the holistic nature of wellness that was understood. In Nehiyawak culture, if someone was ill their entire life and circumstances would be evaluated in an attempt to understand the cause. According to traditional Indigenous medicine, illness could be caused by issues within one of four parts of a being. The Medicine Wheel was created as the traditional model of wellness among many Indigenous Nations. Causes of illness were considered to be more than just physical, for example, emotional or spiritual issues could be a cause.

The Medicine Wheel has four equal parts which make up the whole circle, the four parts correspond to the four directions: north, east, south, and west. Typically, the north is associated with the color white, east with yellow, south with red, and west with black or sometimes dark blue. Each part of the wheel is representative of an aspect of health, and together they create a holistic view of a person and their health. The north is the spiritual side of a person, the east is physical, the south is mental, and the west is emotional.

When a person is viewed as a whole and within the context of their environment, community, and circumstances, the causes and remedies of illness are understood differently than in the western world, where only the physical aspects are considered. In the traditional Indigenous view of wellness, someone with a seemingly physically-based wound or illness would be evaluated or considered in the context of their emotional, spiritual, and mental well-being. For example, if the ill person is mourning loss-making emotions and spirituality out of balance, that could be a reason for the illness; it would also inform the methods of treatment. To heal the spiritual wounds, the person might need to attend a sweat, a pipe ceremony, or a drumming circle. This helps the person integrate with their spirituality and allows healing to begin.

The holistic view of health as encompassing more than just the physical symptom of a disease is profound. The idea that spirituality and emotions are an integral part of overall health is slowly becoming more accepted in western medicine. It is now known to western doctors and health practitioners that mental health plays a big role in the overall well-being of a patient. The Indigenous holistic views of health have always attended to that reality. Interesting how that ancient knowledge and awareness was more sustainable and accurate than the western views that have attempted to replace it over the past 200 years.

Nehiyawak and the Effects of Colonialism

Nehiyawak people first encountered Europeans in the late 1600s in the vast and densely forested wilderness that is now called the Hudson Bay.

Trappers and missionaries who had encountered other Indigenous Nations on the east coast were traveling westward to explore the rest of the continent when the Nehiyawak first made contact with them.

The relationship began, as most Indigenous-European ones did, with the Nehiyawak Nation welcoming the Europeans into their territory. Nehiyawak bands began to trade with European explorers and trappers to help them learn the way of the land, which most Europeans at the time were not familiar with.

As the demand for fur in Europe continued during the late 1600s and into the 1700s, the fur trade grew, and the interactions and relationships between Nehiyawak bands and the fur traders increased. The fur traders began establishing more permanent settlements in the Nehiyawak territory, including in the Hudson

Bay area and beyond.

Some bands felt that they benefited from the fur trade with Europeans and were motivated to migrate or stay in that area to continue to trade, and many of them eventually chose to integrate more with the settlers. Because the Nehiyawak had always been a migratory and band-based nation—with networks and marriages happening between bands and cultures for time immemorial—it was natural for them to be more open to cross-cultural learning and relationships.

Whereas other bands were not as comfortable with the fur trade or with the growing numbers of settlers in the area; many of these bands relocated westward into the prairies. The Nehiyawak who migrated west from the forest to the prairies had to adapt to the new environment, they quickly learned many new skills such as buffalo hunting and traveling on horseback.

Many of the European settlements had missions from various Christian orders that operated churches, schools, and health services. Many Indigenous people were open to this new type of spirituality, learning, and health care and voluntarily integrated into the settlements through the missions. By integrating cultures and communities, an entirely new and distinct culture was born; the new culture consisted of families with an Indigenous mother and a French settler father. As cross-cultural relationships became common, the families banded together to form a distinct culture called the Métis Nation.

Treaties became a critical factor in Indigenous and Euro-settler relations in the 1800s. At first, they were allegedly created in an effort to settle disputes and the question of land ownership and land use rights. Treaties significantly impacted the Indigenous way of life for the Nehiyawak people. It was particularly impactful to the traditional migration-based lifestyle to be confined to such a small space.

Many Indigenous communities, especially across the prairies, were coerced into signing the treaties as colonizers withheld supplies or other resources from them if they did not cooperate. Other bands and groups were promised future considerations or protections of their sovereignty if they signed treaty agreements.

Although the intended outcome of the treaties in the prairies was allegedly to limit interactions and conflicts between the Nehiyawak and other nations with Euro-settlers, they had the opposite effect. Around the same time that treaties were being signed, the colonial and settler governments were also making laws against traditional Indigenous cultural practices. The Canadian and American governments also created new policing systems at that time to keep Indigenous People on the reserve land and prevent the cultural practices that had been banned. This greatly affected the Nehiyawak with their traditional nomadic lifestyle.

Understandably, the treaties and laws only created more tension and conflict between Indigenous Nations and the settlers. Again, in a further misguided attempt to mitigate the conflicts, the government decided that Indigenous children should be assimilated into the Settler-Canadian culture by forced attendance in the "residential schools." Especially across the prairies, the government also enforced attendance at the schools through the newly created policing system, the Royal

Canadian Mounted Police. Children were forcibly removed from their families and communities and brought to the "residential schools" against anyone's wishes and without consent. Tragically, as mentioned in the previous section, many children never returned home, and their families were never notified of what happened to them; most families were left to mourn and wonder what horrible fate had become their children forever. Those that did return were never to be the same. The amount of abuse and neglect they faced caused generational trauma that profoundly affects all Indigenous people.

Even though the "residential schools" are now closed and some other advancements for Indigenous rights have been made, there is still a lot of injustice and racism against Indigenous people in North America. Both systemic and overt racism continues to inhibit and affect Indigenous Peoples today, not to mention the lingering effects of the trauma that has impacted many generations. A lot of racism the Indigenous people are currently facing is systemic. Such things as the quantifiably poorer health outcomes for Indigenous people can be attributed in many ways to systemic racism; due to a lack of accessible health care resources, being dismissed and not heard or believed by healthcare professionals, and even from such seemingly basic barriers like a lack of potable water on reserves.

The Haudenosaunee (Iroquois) Confederacy in the Northeast

The Haudenosaunee Confederacy, more commonly known as the Iroquois Confederacy, is a coalition of six Indigenous groups who created a powerful league of peaceful and cooperative nations. It is unclear exactly when the five founding Nations established the confederacy, although oral Haudenosaunee history suggests that it may have existed in some form as early as the mid-1100s. However, that fact is disputed by western scientists who argue that the archaeological evidence dates back to the mid-1400s.

The Nations of the Haudenosaunee Confederacy occupied the Northeastern region of the United States, mostly, what would be considered New England in the present day, and north from there into Southern Canada. Initially, the Confederacy members were the Kanien'kehá:ka (Mohawk), OnΛyoteʔa·ká (Oneida), Onoñda'gega' (Onondaga), Gayogǫhó:nǫ' (Cayuga), Onödowa'ga:' (Seneca). Later, in 1722, the Skarù·rę? (Tuscarora) people joined. The confederacy was known to the European fur traders and settlers as the Six Nations.

It is said that the Confederacy was created as a peace agreement between five founding

Indigenous Nations. The peace agreement called The Great Law of Peace was expressed as a principle by a visionary leader and medicine man, Deganawida, The Great Peacemaker. It's not clear exactly what his life was like or from which nation he originated. He met Hiawatha, a great and legendary leader from the Onondaga and Mohawk peoples. It's not an exaggeration to say that their meeting and relationship impacted the lives of millions of people throughout history. They discussed the philosophy of peace and laid out the principles of The Great Law of Peace. It is rare in history that two people so visionary and pure of the heart come together to make political decisions. They were true philosopher-kings who led with the genuine intention of bettering the social and political world of the Haudenosaunee Peoples.

The two men gathered leaders from five nations who were feuding for centuries to agree on peace. At that time, the nations worked together to create the Gayanashagowa (Great Law of Peace). It was customary for records to be kept in the form of beaded sash-like creations called wampum. That is how their history was held, through the oral tradition of passing on stories from one generation to the next, which were aided by the wampum.

The agreement that the Nations came to is similar to a modern-day constitution; it outlined members' expectations and responsibilities, the scopes of power of the leaders, and how leaders would be selected and removed. According to Alaka Wali, the constitution of the Haudenosaunee Confederacy included these tenets that are now well recognized as key features of successful democracies (Wali, A., 2016):

- A restriction on holding dual offices

- Processes to remove chiefs from the confederacy leadership
- A multi-level legislature with procedures in place for passing laws
- A method of how and when to declare war
- According to later transcriptions, the creation of a balance of power between the Iroquois Confederacy and individual tribes.

The Grand Council of the Haudenosaunee Confederacy consisted of about 50 chief representatives; initially, there were 14 chiefs from the Onondaga, 10 from the Cayuga, nine chiefs each from the Oneida and the Mohawk Nations. When the Tuscarora joined, they were non-voting members. All decisions had to be made by a unanimous consensus, and when members brought matters to the Grand Council for lawmaking, each Nation had a role in considering the case. First, an issue would be considered by the Seneca and Mohawk chiefs, after which they would pass it on, along with their thoughts, to the Oneida and Cayuga Chiefs for further deliberation. Finally, the Onondaga Chiefs were the final decision-makers of the process. They would hear what the others had to say and ensure a unanimous consensus before turning any matter into law. This system was the most thorough way to ensure democracy was served and to avoid an imbalance of power in the hands of just one individual chief or nation.

Although this Confederacy was not the first or last, it is the most enduring. The Haudenosaunee Confederacy is now known to be the longest-running democratic system globally. Several factors appear to have set this confederacy apart from others; it was well defined and well organized with a complex electoral system that included checks and balances. These factors seem to have made the coalition generally more effective and, in turn, more enduring than any other.

Because each Nation was made up of several community groups, each group was then made up of several clans, ensuring that all people were adequately represented was complicated. The Confederacy uses a unique and complex electoral system based on the matrilineal principles typical of many Indigenous peoples, including those of the Haudenosaunee Confederacy.

The Haudenosaunee culture was matrilineal. Each family had a designated Clan Mother, who was traditionally the eldest female family member, although now she is generally chosen by consensus because of her devotion to the traditional culture and family. Each family lived in a communal longhouse, grouped through the women's relations. When people married, traditionally the man would move into his wife's family's longhouse and no matter where he lived, he would always retain his original membership to his mother's clan.

The Clan Mother of each family was responsible for selecting the clan chief called the Hoyaneh, who was always a man. The Clan Mother also had the power to remove Hoyaneh from their positions if she felt he was not properly representing the clan. Aside from selecting the Hoyaneh, the Clan Mother was responsible for naming the members of the clan, ensuring that everyone was cared for and well-fed, and making many decisions for the clan.

At the time that they joined forces, the Nations that made up the Confederacy were agriculturists and predominantly sedentary. They were relatively early adopters of farming practices and grew what is known as the three sister crops: corn, beans, and squash, which were the earliest and prominent subsistence crops grown by Indigenous Peoples in the Americas. Cultivating the three sisters offered many benefits to the Haudenosaunee Confederacy, including a relatively reliable food source that they could have a greater degree of control over. With the consistency of an agriculture-based society, came a more sedentary lifestyle, which revolved around the crops and the work to tend them.

The agricultural lifestyle was relatively relaxed for the Haudenosaunee people. The men cleared fields in early spring and the women and older children spent most of the spring and summer seeding and tending to the crops. Men would be busy with hunting and other seasonal tasks during those months, which included building and repairing houses.

After the transition to agriculture, the

Haudenosaunee people built permanent shelters and started living in one place year-round. The houses they built were called longhouses, and the name Haudenausonee means the "People of the Longhouse." The switch to agriculture and sedentary living freed up time formerly spent migrating and repeatedly reestablishing shelters and camps. The Haudenosaunee lifestyle was relatively relaxed as a result, and the people were well cared for, including any enslaved laborers that the Haudenosaunee took during wars.

The transition to agriculture occurred before the confederacy of the Haudenosaunee Nations was formed. During the time before the coalition was established, nations fought over hunting and gathering territories and other issues that arose from occupying neighboring territories. They would often take war prisoners from each other to enslave as laborers as well as to adopt as replacements for dead relatives. As the formerly nomadic nations settled into permanent settlements, it became more desirable and efficient to have peace. It also helped to create more safety in a larger group if necessary.

Before the arrival of the Europeans, the traditional rivals of the Haudenosaunee were the Huron, the Mohicans, and at times other neighboring nations. The prime motive of war at that time was to take captives for enslaved labor and protect or take over hunting territory. Largely because of the demand for enslaved laborers, the Haudenosaunee did not glorify killing their rivals in battle. They also profoundly valued the lives of their own people and strove to minimize the loss of warriors as much as possible.

In the Haudenosaunee culture, grieving was a very important aspect of spirituality. Family and friends deeply mourned those who passed, especially in battle. There were many sacred rituals that attended to the grieving process and honored the dead. The first was the condolences ceremony, where attendees were divided into two groups, the first was the most directly affected who were mourning, and the second group was the relations who were less directly affected, and they were the comforting group. The nation of the deceased hosts the condolence ceremony unless there were special circumstances or reasons that they could not, in which case it would be hosted by another nation. The members of the other nations would come to visit and offer condolences and comfort to the nation of the deceased. If the deceased was a chief, then a replacement would often be chosen at the same time and appointed.

Another traditional grieving practice of the Haudenosaunee was the revenge-seeking mourning-wars. If a warrior or chief died in battle, it was customary for the clan and nation to seek revenge in the form of a mourning war. The mourning nation would raid and attack the rival village to kidnap hostages. Once the mourners took the hostages and brought them back to their own village, they tortured them ritualistically.

The torture was a communal practice that involved participation from everyone in the community, including children. Communal torture like this was not unique to the Haudenosaunee nations, in fact, it was typical for all Indigenous Nations in the northeast woodlands during the time period. The length and severity of the torture reflected the mother's grief from the loss; if the loss was particularly painful and the mother was particularly bereaved, the torture would be more severe. It was a vengeful and cathartic practice.

After the torture, there were two outcomes that could become of the captive. The first, yet less common, the outcome was simply death. The second was a form of adoption into the mourning family, as a replacement for the member who was lost. The mourning mother would decide to either keep the captive as a member of her clan, to replace the one who was lost, or to kill the captive.

Generally, the captives were adopted as the Haudenosaunee didn't believe in unnecessary death. The traditional belief was that when a member was lost, the group lost some power and became weaker. For that reason, the clans adopted a replacement member. Once the replacement was brought into the family they generally stayed and became a member of the group.

Although war and torture were a part of the

Haudenosaunee culture for a long time, through the confederacy the Gayanesshagowa, the Great Law of Peace, it was a major goal of the Haudenosaunee to try to find peace among themselves and with all other peoples. The Gayanesshagowa outlined many ways for conflicting nations to recognize the suffering of one another and to attempt to alleviate the loss of lives and resulting suffering.

One of the most sacred and renowned ceremonies associated with the Gayanashagowa is the Great Tree of Peace. When the confederacy was born, the nations planted a white pine and buried their weapons beneath it. This symbolized leaving war and weapons behind and growing a better, less violent, and traumatic future together. It became a symbol that was used with other nations as well, including with the Europeans when they began exploring the eastern part of the continent.

The Haudenosaunee and European Contact

When the Europeans arrived, the fur trade and the weapons that came with them created a shift in the dynamic that had been established between the Haudenosaunee and their neighboring tribes, the Huron and Algonquians. Alliances were formed between the various Indigenous Nations and the various European traders.

The Haudenosaunee were sought-after trading partners and allies for the recently landed Europeans. Their territory was well located on the eastern seaboard, and they controlled a large part of the land.

Perhaps the most notorious aspect of Haudenosaunee and European contact is the series of conflicts known as the French-Iroquois Wars or the Beaver Wars. These wars have gone down in history as some of the bloodiest wars in American history. It's hard to imagine that these wars were fought over beavers, for that matter, it's hard to believe that most of the conflict between the Indigenous Nations and the Europeans was for such frivolous and passing trends.

The first contact between the Haudenosaunee and the French occurred in 1609. Early relations were strained between the two peoples due to Samuel de Champlain killing three Haudenosaunee chiefs. This, of course, created a rivalry and adversarial relationship from the beginning. They continued to battle on and off until the 1700s.

At that time, the Dutch and the Haudenosaunee were the main trading partners in the fur trade.

The Haudenosaunee controlled the largest territory on the Northeast coast with plenty of beaver habitat. They had the advantage of good supply and strong trade with the Dutch who were initially the largest purchasers of beaver pelts in the area.

What further strained the relationship between all groups in the Northeast, Indigenous and European was the rapid depletion of the beavers in the area. With the high demand of beaver pelts for trade and the introduction of European firearms to the Indigenous Nations of the Northeast, including the Haudenosaunee, the beaver population quickly declined. As beavers became less available, the Haudenosaunee sought to take more land in order to maintain control of the fur trade. They began to fight wars to expand their territory and ended up displacing other tribes who were forced to relocate further west.

Wars and conflicts continued as the European nations also fought each other for control of the fur trade, land use, and resources. As European settlements became more common and more permanent, especially along the eastern seaboard and the main river junctions inland, the settlers wanted more control over the territory. The Haudenosaunee Confederacy became the main representation of the tribes in the Northeast, including the six-member tribes, but they also included and negotiated on behalf of several more tribes. The strong and well-established confederacy was a great benefit to all Indigenous Nations in the area as it united and amplified the voices that only gained power from being aggregated and otherwise would have been completely defeated and dominated by the European forces and settlers.

After nearly a century of conflict in the

Northeast, a peace agreement was made between the Haudenosaunee, the French, and the English. The French occupied the area to the North of the Haudenosaunee territory, and the English occupied the South. The Haudenosaunee territory created a buffer zone between the two rivals, and they were able to trade and create relationships with both colonies.

The peaceful period did not last long and by the early 1700s, the Haudenosaunee population had declined considerably due to war and to the newly introduced European diseases. With the peace in the area, European colonies were growing quickly, and they were soon trying to push their territory boundaries into the Haudenosaunee land, which created a new spark in conflict.

In the mid-1700s the French and Indian War

was fought. It was a multifaceted battle that had several warring sides. The Haudenosaunee sided with the British who had been their allies for many decades at that point and with whom they had a functional if not beneficial relationship. The other warring parties included the French to the North, who were backed by the Algonquian Nation. Following this war, the British continued to reward the Haudenosaunee by signing land treaties for use as Confederacy reserve land and would be protected and held under their control. The amount of land that was lawfully and practically Haudenosaunee territory during the 1700s was sizable. However, over the following decades, the Haudenosaunee gradually ceded large quantities back to the British.

The next conflict that disrupted the peace for the Haudenosaunee and the entire "New World" was the American Revolution. The Haudenosaunee attempted to remain neutral in the conflict between the settled Americans and the British Empire. To the Haudenosaunee, the two groups were not distinct, and they failed to fully understand what the conflict was about. They viewed all the English speakers as one united group. They also didn't want to choose a side because they had a good working relationship with both the British and the Americans. Eventually, due to their long history of trade and allyship, the Confederacy was pressured to support the British.

This war is ultimately what ended up disbanding the Confederacy as not all the Nation members were supportive of the British. Each Nation of the Confederacy ended up going their own way at this point and the Alliance ended. The American Revolution affected the nations of the Haudenosaunee greatly, leaving them with many more casualties and villages destroyed by war. After the war ended, the lifestyle and quality of life for Indigenous

Nations began to decline more steadily.

The general tension between Indigenous peoples and settlers increased as the sense of domination and oppression increased. There were more treaties being signed and they were being more strictly enforced. After the Revolution, the new governments of Canada and the United States started to create more laws to prohibit the practice and expression of Indigenous culture and traditions. The former members of the Haudenosaunee Confederacy, like all Indigenous people in the US and Canada, were also subjected to forceful and unconsented removal of children who were then placed in "residential schools" where many perished or disappeared.

Although the treaties stated that Indigenous People, especially those whose traditional territory straddled the American-Canadian border, had the right to travel between the two countries and purchase or bring goods across without paying duties; it took a long time and a lot of activism for these rights to be recognized. Over time more rights have been recognized but it was not without a fight, and not without grave harm and trauma caused by the discrimination and oppression. Such is the way with most aspects of rights and freedoms for Indigenous people in the Americas, and indeed across the globe.

The Choctaw Nation in the Southeast

The Choctaw Nation traditionally inhabited a large territory in the Southeastern United States, where it is now Oklahoma, Alabama, Mississippi, and Louisiana. The Choctaw language, Chohta, is considered a part of the Western Muskogean Languages and is the native language of nearly 10,000 people living in the United States. There are several tribes that make up the Choctaw Nation and each has its own distinct stories and history. As with all Indigenous Nations included in this book, this is a generalized account of the history, as each specific Nation, tribe, clan, family, and even individual would have their own accounts of what life was.

The Choctaw are descended from the Mound Building peoples who populated what is now southeastern North America for over 5,000 years. Archaeological evidence places the Mound Builders at several sites, the Choctaw descended from the Mississippian Mound Builders, which was the third and final era or stage of the Mound Building Culture. Mound Building cultures had developed hierarchical social structures with an elite or ruling class and a subordinate or laboring class. This represented a certain level of sophistication and complexity in social organization that would have evolved in a stable group over a long time. It indicates a long history as a people that organized in complex ways over time. This type of social structure can only happen as population size increases due to the agrarian and sedentary lifestyle.

The Mound Builder cultures used the labor of the lower-class members to create impressive earthen mound structures. The mounds generally had four sides and were leveled on the top to be a platform, like a flat-topped pyramid constructed with compressed dirt. The laborers who built the mounds would excavate the dirt from one site and transport it in baskets to the mound site, they would then dump the dirt onto the mound and trample it down by foot. Eventually, the mounds would take shape into a large, often tiered platform structure. Sometimes more tiers would be added at later times from the original construction.

Although they had various purposes, each mound was sacred; some were used as a burial site for chiefs or other important members of the group, others were extravagant platforms for the chief's dwelling, others were used as political places where groups would gather to discuss trade and other diplomatic issues.

Like many Indigenous Nations, the Choctaw Nation was divided into two groups or moieties. Each moiety consisted of three districts and each district had several clans with each clan consisting of several groups who occupied their own towns and villages. The Choctaw society was complex and well organized with many levels of leadership and governance. The chiefs of the districts were called mingos and were chosen for having strong characteristics and leadership abilities which included a history of military achievement, good ancestry, good organization, and ability to communicate well. This system ensured that the Choctaws were governed in a democratic way and that all people were adequately considered and represented.

Marriages were only allowed to happen between moieties. Following the matrilineal tradition, children were considered a part of the moiety and clan from which their mother originated.

The Choctaw were an agrarian and sedentary people from a relatively early point in the history of Indigenous Nations in the Americas, as evident from their descending from the Mississippian Mound Builders. They produced the staple three sisters' crops of corn, beans, and squash.

Like all Indigenous Peoples, the Choctaw's

lifestyle was seasonal and revolved around what was necessary and possible to do in each distinct time of the year. Chores and tasks were also divided by gender roles and between classes in the hierarchical society.

Traditionally, the new year began at the spring equinox; at that time most of the people, regardless of gender and age, would participate in sowing the seeds for the sustenance crops. From that point on, it was mainly the women and children who tended to the crops, ensuring they were watered and weeded throughout the increasingly hot months of summer.

In spring, while the women and children were occupied in the fields, the men would go hunt and trap small game such as rabbits, wild hogs, turkeys, and any other available protein sources. The women would process the meat to be prepared for eating and the men would process and tan the hides, rendering them useful for making clothes, blankets, and other essentials.

Over the summer, tending the crops continued to be the main priority and kept most of the women and children busy. When the crops were ripened at the end of summer it was time for a sacred celebration of life and the gifts of harvest. The celebrations included a deeply spiritual aspect, and the participants would pray and fast to focus on forgiveness and new beginnings. This was the main spiritual and cultural event of the year.

During the fall, hunting large game became the focus for the Choctaw men. They hunted deer, bears, and other large animals. The women would focus on processing the meat. A major celebration event occurred late in the fall, before winter when things became quieter, and people spent more time making crafts and telling stories.

The Choctaw women and men were skilled crafters who were renowned for their woven baskets made from river cane, pottery from river clay, shell jewelry and beads, as well as fine fabric made from mulberry bark. Winter was a good time for crafting as it provided a natural break from the field and agriculture-related labor.

Building houses and other necessary structures was another occupation that employed the labor of both women and men. The houses were permanent structures, traditionally constructed with heavy posts and beams made from locally and intentionally harvested lumber. The men were responsible for providing and setting the heavy posts and frame of the house. The women would then complete the structure by adding mud and grass in a specialized technique to fill in the walls. The roofs were made from thatched river grasses and later covered in tree bark as well.

Most men were also warriors and athletes who trained hard year-round to provide protection for the villages. The Choctaw people were known as peaceful people, raiding was not a part of their culture. However, they did maintain an active and well-trained warrior force that focused more on defensive tactics than raiding or attacking. As such, it was the philosophy that the warriors must be very skillful in order to appropriately defend women and children in their own territory and villages.

Ishtaboli, or stickball in English, which is a traditional Indigenous sport played by many Indigenous Nations, was a big part of the Choctaw culture as well. Ishtaboli was played using sticks with woven baskets on the end to catch and throw the ball, the ball must hit a goal post situated at either end of a long-playing field in order for the team to score. It is the origin sport of Lacrosse which is gaining popularity today.

Ishtaboli was played by the men in the Choctaw tribe, they put a lot of time and energy into training for the sport. Ishtaboli was very competitive with many nations competing against each other in big matches and tournaments which could include hundreds of players or more and have thousands of spectators. The game rules were relatively elaborate, players each portrayed and embodied an animal spirit in their costume and sporting style. Ishtaboli was also extremely physical, with many injuries and even deaths occurring as a result. The skills and athletics learned from playing Ishtaboli were used as a form of training for the warriors of the tribe.

Traditionally the Choctaw played many other games as pastimes and entertainment and not all were as physical as Ishtaboli. Other games included one that used painted seeds in a similar way to dice throwing and another where objects would be hidden in shells.

The Choctaw and European Contact

Because the Choctaw were situated near the Atlantic on the Southeast side of North America, they were one of the first Indigenous nations to have contact with the European explorers in the early 1500s. At this time, they were subjected to all of the diseases that plagued Indigenous People from the time the Europeans arrived and the population declined significantly.

It was the Spaniards who first encountered the Choctaw and took a mingo hostage. The

Spaniards demanded that the Choctaw give them resources such as canoes, laborers, and women in exchange for the return of the chief. Tuscaloosa, the kidnapped mingo, escaped and refused to release the laborers and women. A battle ensued in which an entire Choctaw village was burned, and hundreds of Choctaw people were killed, as well as two dozen Spaniards.

It wasn't until the 1700s that the French began to establish permanent colonial settlements and trading posts in Choctaw territory along the Mississippi River. Due to their naturally peaceful nature and formally established villages and societal structure, the Choctaw were early allies and trading partners with the French, however, the impact of European contact remained relatively minor for the most part.

It wasn't until the 1800s when American contact

gradually became more frequent and affected the Choctaw People. Due to encroaching American villages and treaties, the Choctaw eventually ceded most of their territory in Mississippi to the Americans in exchange for land and freedom in Oklahoma. The majority of Choctaw moved westward into Oklahoma, with some also settling in Texas at that time.

The Choctaw remained peaceful and open to interactions with Americans but even so, eventually, the Americans began to establish more and more so-called "anti-Indian" laws and practices to try to eliminate Indigenous culture and to "civilize" the people. Finally in the mid-1800s after several hundred years of relatively peaceful coexistence with the white man, the Choctaw fought back. The battle lasted two days and was not victorious for the Choctaw. Many Choctaw escaped to Mexico at that time or joined other tribes in Oklahoma.

To this day the effects of the American "anti-Indian" sentiment can be felt and observed. As history and traditions were lost when the lineage of the oral tradition and practice was interrupted. Sadly, many of the Indigenous Nations in the southern United States were also subjected to the "residential schools" designed to civilize the Indigenous Peoples in America. The trauma of families being separated lasted for several generations and continues to affect the lives of hundreds of thousands of people today.

The Ben 'Zaa (Zapotec) People of Southwestern Mexico

The Ben 'Zaa is the name by which the Zapotec people now self-identify. Ben 'Zaa means the cloud people and they call themselves that because they believed that the clouds were the divine beings from which they were created and that upon death they would return to the clouds. The Ben 'Zaa is more commonly known as the Zapotec people and is made up of several groups who shared the Zapotec culture and civilization. They are a large Indigenous group who have occupied the Oaxaca region in southwestern Mexico for millennia, where they were dominant and well established from as early as 1100 B.C.E. The Indigenous language was called Zapotecan and included a written form that used glyphs from an early time in history.

The Zapotecs established complex permanent villages and cities, with the largest and most enduring being Monte Albán, which was known as the political center or capital of the Zapotec civilization. Monte Albán was heavily fortified, indicating that there was many conflicts and many battles in Zapotec history requiring the overall need for defense in the time and place that the city was built. The walls of the fortified city were adorned with many stone slabs with carved images depicting military victory and power, as well as the terrible outcomes for the war captives from rival groups. It was indeed an impressive and intimidating city that provoked both awe and submission.

Monte Albán was an elaborate city and shows the overall level of social organization and sophistication of the Zapotec people at the time. The city included elaborate architecture that was laid out with both intention and attention to detail in perfect north-south lines. The sophisticated urban design plans included dams and canals to provide access to water, gymnasiums for sports and games, religious temples and burial sites, elegant dwellings for the upper class, common dwellings alongside as well as open communal space. The stone buildings and walls of the city were all skillfully and elaborately carved, illustrating both the opulence and the appreciation of art in the Zapotec culture. The remains of Monte Albán are impressive, and the site is recognized as a UNESCO World Heritage site that draws visitors from all over the world.

If Monte Albán was the political and economic center of the ancient Ben 'Zaa civilization, then Mitlá was considered the religious capital. The name Mitlá is a Hispanicised variation of the word Mictlan, which means a resting place for the dead. The city was completely ornate, and it is clear and easy to observe how much work went into building it with every structure decorated with beautiful and elaborately patterned masonry. The city was believed to be the earthly gateway to the afterlife in the clouds and was used as the burial site for the Zapotec elite to ensure that they would be returned to the clouds.

For those Zapotecs who were not of the elite ruling class, it was believed that they originated in caves and were somehow descended from the jaguar and puma which both played central roles in mythology and religion. The common Zapotecs had different burial practices and ceremonies from the elite. Many were buried with their prized possessions beneath the floor of the family home so that they could return to the earth and still be able to communicate with their family, in this way the ancestors remained a sacred part of the Zapotec family.

Other traditional religious ceremonies included sacrificial offerings of animals and at times even humans. The sacrifices, which often included removing a beating heart, were made as offerings to the Gods in an attempt to influence and persuade them to improve conditions that were out of human control. Often the sacrifices were made to Cocijo who was the Zapotec god of storms and rain.

The Zapotec civilization was highly organized and specialized, much like society today, with people occupying many specific roles. There were elites who ruled and governed at various levels, then the majority of the population who filled functional roles in the society such as potters, theists, linguists and scribes, builders, masons and sculptors, jewelers who crafted fine pieces from gold, athletes, agricultural food producers, and so on.

The most popular Zapotec sport, as evidenced by the arenas built into the cities, was known as a ballgame. The location of the ballgame arenas in the central and religious areas of the cities indicates that the sport was a very important aspect of the Zapotec culture. The game was played in a similar way to soccer as it involved moving a ball between players by only using feet and scoring points by passing the ball through goalposts. The ball was much harder, and the sport may have been rougher between players than soccer is today. The Zapotec players wore more protective gear to avoid injuries from getting hit with the ball. There are many depictions of ballgames being played in Zapotec and Mayan art, including on ceramics and in stone carving. Some of the depictions of the matches end in a ceremonial sacrifice. There is still a version of this game played in the Oaxaca region of Mexico today.

Zapotecan was also a highly evolved language and included a written form that used glyphs to represent each syllable of a word. The glyphs were used to record history and keep records and are believed to be the oldest written language of Mesoamerica. The Zapotecs also developed and used a calendar system to track the passage of time according to cycles of the moon and seasons.

At the height of their power, the Zapotecs were

actively expanding and dominating villages and cities beyond the Oaxaca territory, creating a massive empire that is estimated to have reached over 500,000 people. The effects of the expansion and domination can be observed in the archaeological records as styles of pottery and art-making suddenly changed as the Zapotecs overtook each village.

The Zapotecs and European Contact

Unfortunately for the Indigenous Peoples of Mesoamerica, it was the Spaniards who first explored the area with the intent to discover and colonize. The Spaniards had a less diplomatic approach to colonization than the French and English did in the same era. Whereas the French and English initially sought to trade with and learn from the Indigenous Peoples they encountered, the Spaniards were known as more ruthless colonizers; they killed as many Indigenous People as possible and tried to conquer and wipe out the cultures as much as possible.

Right around the time that the Europeans were first exploring the region now known as Mexico, the Zapotecs were engaged in a series of battles with the Aztecs. The Aztecs were becoming the dominant force between the two although they had yet to conquer the Zapotecs.

Shortly after the final battle between the Zapotecs and the Aztecs, the Spaniards arrived. They first encountered the Incas and Aztecs. Like the other European explorers and traders, The Spanish conquistadors spread diseases throughout the Indigenous villages, immediately lowering the populations and limiting their ability to adequately defend themselves. The Aztecs and Incas were the first of the Mesoamerican civilizations to be conquered by the Spaniards.

Having heard this news, the Zapotecs, hoping for a more diplomatic outcome, attempted to avoid the same fate by avoiding attacking the Spaniards. The tactic did not work and ultimately the diseases and the conquistadors decimated the Zapotecs as well. After the Spaniards conquered Mexico, very few Indigenous People remained alive and many of those who did survive were ill-fated to become enslaved by the Spanish colonies.

CHAPTER 6
CONTEMPORARY ISSUES OF TREATIES AND LAND USE

In the minds of most North Americans, particularly those who are descendants of settlers, colonialism is over. This is likely because the present-day nations that dominate, occupy, and govern the land and people of North America are so well established. For Indigenous People, however, colonialism continues, as their rights and sovereignty continue to be encroached upon.

Much of the conflict that remains between Indigenous Nations and settler governments stems from the cultural differences in the meaning of some of the agreements made. The fundamental differences in views meant that even though each nation believed that they were understanding each other and signing a treaty or agreement that had the same meaning for each party, the truth is, they weren't. The underlying beliefs about the meaning of the agreements were completely different without either party realizing the impact that would have on the way that the treaties were put into practice. The differing views are described in the Canadian Encyclopedia:

> On the one hand, is the government's view of treaties as legal instruments that surrendered Indigenous rights. On the other is the Indigenous view of treaties as

instruments of relationships between autonomous peoples who agree to share the lands and resources of Canada. Seen from the Indigenous perspective, treaties do not surrender rights; rather, they confirm Indigenous rights. Treaties recognize that Indigenous peoples have the capacity to self-govern. Bridging the gap between these two views of treaties poses a huge challenge to people and lawmakers in Canada. (Hall, 2017, para 7)

Due to the lack of cultural understanding between the Indigenous Nations and the settler governments, it seems that in the eyes of the settlers the Indigenous Nations had signed away more rights than they believed they had. Subsequently, when the governments began using more force to attempt to control and enforce the treaties and "anti-Indian laws," it created more conflict between the Indigenous

Nations and the governments.

There is a major imbalance of power in the relationship between Indigenous Nations and contemporary colonial governments. This imbalance stems from many factors including the long history of racist attitudes and policies toward Indigenous Peoples and their cultures, as well as the relatively small population of Indigenous People and the dispersion of the Indigenous population on remote reserves across the continent.

Although most Indigenous Nations are supportive of each other and advocate for common rights and sovereignty, each nation faces its own unique forms of oppression which demand its own resources and energy to fight. This makes it challenging to unify as one powerful voice since much energy and focus and attention must be used on regional issues.

Coupled with the lack of amplification, is also a general lack of power and resources to properly assert rights and maintain sovereignty when and if the governments of the larger colonial nations choose to overstep their bounds. This also makes it next to impossible for Indigenous Nations to participate in the so-called democratic resolutions that the colonial powers consider essential to resolving the issues (the legal system). There is no reason, besides colonial egoism and self-appointed power, that the contemporary issues between Indigenous Nations and colonial governments or other landowners should not be resolved according to traditional Indigenous ways as opposed to being decided by a colonial judge in the Western fashion.

These issues are compounded by the generational lack of access to education in the colonial systems, leaving Indigenous People and Indigenous Nations under-represented and misunderstood by the majority of colonial descendants or participants in the contemporary colonial societies. What makes the lack of access to education worse is the tragic history of "residential schools" which caused immeasurable trauma and likely irreparable mistrust of not only the colonial school system, social services, and policing, but of all other forms of colonial authorities.

What further complicates the matter and makes it difficult for Indigenous Nations to use their potential collective power is that across each country and across each region within those countries, the treaties and rights that may be in place are different. While some nations and groups have no treaties whatsoever, others have clearly defined treaties that work for them, and others still have treaties that were written over 300 years ago and may not reflect the reality of what is happening or needed in the present day. In the case of these old treaties, we must also question the validity of the treaty and how well informed and understanding the people were who signed the treaties. The issues that are arising for Indigenous Nations are all somewhat unique and create fragmentation in the fight for equality.

The truth of the matter is that none of this should matter. The truth is that Indigenous People should not have to fight for their rights to maintain the sovereignty of their territories. The only reason that most Indigenous Nations still have to defend those rights is that the deep-seated racism of colonialism still exists, and although there are treaties that recognize the rights of Indigenous People and Indigenous Nations, the majority of politicians and governments in North America do not. There is still a pervasive and damaging view that Indigenous culture, values, and land use practices are somehow inherently less valid than colonial ways of being and operating. This is likely only because Indigenous culture is not based on capitalism, whereas Western views only see value in something if it is monetized. Indigenous Nations' rights to sovereignty are often respected by governments until there is a motivation or a reason to monetize the land and resources, in which case that need to monetize by default becomes more important than anything that Indigenous Nations are doing there. Governments have a tendency to appropriate land or otherwise override treaty rights and Indigenous Nations sovereignty when they have a monetary incentive of some kind to do so.

Environmental Racism

Another form of systemic racism faced by many Indigenous Nations is environmental racism which has been prevalent since the settlers arrived. Environmental racism can show up in such ways as landfills built on or directly beside Indigenous reserve land or pollutants dumped into waterways on or adjacent to Indigenous Nations communities. This type of racism continues to be extremely physically and mentally harmful to Indigenous Nations people, as is the gaslighting efforts to make believe that it is not discriminatory or race-based decision making that propels these types of decisions.

Environmental racism primarily exists in the form of various levels of government using Indigenous land (or the land adjacent to it) for unwanted and harmful factories or other unsightly usages. For example, if a city wants to build a new landfill rather than situating the landfill in an area where white settlers live, they will use the land on or near a reserve instead. This amounts to the "not in my backyard mentality" where more wealthy and privileged groups of society export their waste and harm to poorer and otherwise disadvantaged groups. The same thing happens globally, where richer countries will have goods produced in poorer countries and leave them with harmful waste and pollution to deal with.

Examples of this can be seen across the continent and over the entire history of colonization. This excerpt from an article by Sezin Koehler (Koehler, 2017) describes a historical example of the type of racist practices that used and manipulated the environment to disadvantage and abuse Indigenous peoples:

> While the term environmental racism has only existed for the past few decades, its reality has existed since the beginning of white settler colonialism in the United States and indigenous communities have been particularly victimized by environmental racism.

From 1872 to 1873 the US military went on a targeted campaign to kill millions of buffalo in order to starve Indigenous populations and force them to comply with the newly developing reservation systems. These plots of reservation lands displaced Indigenous communities from their ancestral homes and were often inhospitable environments without easy access to water, food, and other natural resources that made self-sufficiency virtually impossible. Even today, indigenous peoples in America continue to survive ongoing and often daily assaults on their rights to livable spaces.

In the same article, Koehler describes how present-day and ongoing policies continue to affect the health and outcomes of Indigenous peoples in the United States (Koehler, 2017):

Reservation lands are often used by big businesses for the transportation of and also dumping of toxic wastes, which poison what little groundwater there may be and make these areas even less habitable than they already are. Some of the bigger cases of toxic waste dumping and the social repercussions on Native communities have even been brought by various tribes such as the Navajo and Hopi Nations to international fora such as the United Nations and World Health Organization since there is so little being done by America's own government to protect indigenous peoples.

Another big example of this is what is occurring now with pipelines both in the United States and in Canada. Governments are continuing to use Indigenous reserve land, or unceded territory land to build pipelines. Despite the treaties and the vehement protests on the part of Indigenous Nations. These practices deteriorate not only the living environment for people on reserves but the natural environment as a whole.

Indigenous nations have continuously been bullied, marginalized, and treated as second-class citizens. Over the past 500 years, European explorers, traders, settlers, and the newly formed settler nations that they created in North America have continuously dominated Indigenous Nations and used various tactics to acquire land and resources. They have also shown time and again that they do not respect or care about the welfare or sovereignty of Indigenous People by ignoring universal morality along with adamant protests and expressed wishes for sovereignty and land use, even on treaties and unceded territories. To be treated with such disregard repeatedly over time, as Indigenous Peoples have been in North

America by all governments that have been in power in all the countries on the continent, degrades the sense of self-worth.

Environmental racism has caused so many impacts to the culture and lifestyle of Indigenous People; from altering traditional land-use practices such as seasonal migration, to loss of habitat of animals that were once relied upon, to a lack of access to clean water, to degradation of the environment limiting agriculture and hunting, to pollution in the water and on the land.

Sovereignty

Sovereignty is perhaps the most important aspect of Indigenous Peoples' rights and a large part of the discussion and conflicts when it comes to relations between many Indigenous Nations and governments.

What is sovereignty and why is it so important for Indigenous Peoples' rights? Sovereignty refers to a nation's autonomy and its ability to self-govern without interference from other nations or external forces, also known as a right to self-determination. Many Indigenous Nations in North America have been advocating and working toward sovereignty since treaties were first created in the 1600s.

Indigenous Peoples are not Canadian or American, they are a separate political and cultural group who live on the same continent and within the borders of the countries, but they are not part of the country. Their territories and reserves are not part of the dominant settler country. As mentioned above many, but not all, Indigenous Nations have an agreement of some kind with the government, and those that do not are entitled to sovereignty by default, as they have never ceded or agreed to give up any of their rights and freedoms as individual nations. Most have signed agreements to maintain the right to determine how their territory or reserve land is used, including a right to consent to potential resource extraction or other projects like pipelines.

Sovereignty usually comes into question when governments wish to use recognized or unceded traditional Indigenous territories. Much more often than not, settler governments use the Indigenous Peoples' land in whatever way they choose without consulting with or gaining prior consent from Indigenous groups that will be affected. In recent times, this has meant the construction of pipelines through and adjacent to Native Reserves and in such a way that will permanently alter the ecosystem and affect the water supply.

Pipelines have been a major conflict between many Indigenous Nations and the governments that have given rise to much discussion about Indigenous sovereignty in North America. Indigenous Nations are generally opposed to the construction of pipelines because the process of constructing them is very disruptive and harmful to the natural environment, not to mention the risk of leaks and spills which cause further harm. When it comes to governments and multinational companies choosing pathways for the proposed pipelines, in true colonial form, the environmental racism shows itself clearly as they are often proposed to cross on or near Native Reserves or unceded territories.

Both in the United States and in Canada, Indigenous Peoples have been fighting against appropriated land use by the federal governments for the construction of pipelines. These fights are very difficult as the settler legal system is very expensive to participate in and oftentimes the group with the most money will be able to drain the resources for the other groups by stalling and creating more work for their lawyers to do. Oftentimes, the groups with less money are not able to compete in the legal system against the richer corporations or governments, so they are never truly held accountable. This is a bully tactic.

In the past, governments would not have consulted at all with Indigenous Nations about land use, and historically treaties were essentially created and used by settlers and governments to secure their own access to resources. That mentality continued over the past few centuries and would continue today if it were not for strong protests and advocacy for the rights of Indigenous Nations and for international organizations like the United Nations. Up until recently, there was never any mention of proper consultation of the

Indigenous Nations that might be affected by development or extraction on or near their territories. Now, the standard has become a consultation with Indigenous Nations; although in several contemporary cases the consultation led nowhere, and governments went ahead with development regardless of the input of Indigenous Nations.

This is where the question of sovereignty really comes up because in these circumstances it is clear that the governments are interfering with the ability of Indigenous Nations to determine the use of their land and territories. There is much debate nationally and internationally about how to resolve these issues and what the "best practices" are for governments on how to consult with and gain consent for projects that may be affecting Indigenous Nations.

In more recent decades, the United Nations has

been involved in resolving conflicts between Indigenous Peoples and governments. Across the globe, countries that have a colonial history are experiencing similar issues of government dominance and lack of respect for Indigenous rights and freedoms. The dominant colonial powers have a very hard time facing the fact that they have been overstepping boundaries and taking advantage of Indigenous groups for centuries to gain access to resources or lands they want. Now, due to several factors, including being faced with increasing resistance from Indigenous Nations and non-Indigenous protesters, which have become more visible and amplified due to non-commercial or grass-roots media sources on the internet and social media, it has become less acceptable to behave that way and governments are being forced to reflect upon their actions and are starting to be held more accountable.

Originating in 1987, the United Nations (UN)

has created a manual for governments and project managers that outlines the minimum requirements of consultation with Indigenous Nations regarding the use of land that may affect them. This is called Free Prior and Informed Consent (FPIC). Essentially, the FPIC document, which is considered an internationally binding law for members of the United Nations, outlines what it means and when, how, and what is required to provide the proper information to Indigenous Nations. It also outlines how to receive informed consent from Indigenous groups before working on a project. Here is a description of FPIC found on the UN website:

> FPIC is a principle protected by international human rights standards that state, 'all peoples have the right to self-determination and—linked to the right to self-determination'—'all peoples have the right to freely pursue their

economic, social and cultural development'. Backing FPIC is the United Nations Declaration on the Rights of Indigenous Peoples (UNDRIP), the Convention on Biological Diversity, and the International Labour Organization Convention 169, which are the most powerful and comprehensive international instruments that recognize the plights of Indigenous Peoples and defend their rights. (United Nations Department of Economic and Social Affairs Indigenous Peoples, 2016, para 2)

The UNDRIP states clearly that sovereignty and a right to self-determination is a human rights that must be fostered, maintained, and protected. Many Indigenous Peoples, including those in North America, have been taken advantage of and have had their basic human rights trampled by bully colonial states. This is why an international governing system is important as a check and balance to federal powers.

Although UNDRIP, which contains the FPIC principles, is essential as a stepping stone to Indigenous Nations sovereignty, in the eyes of many people, it does not go far enough to truly foster and establish sovereignty and self-determination for Indigenous groups. The document describes informed consent, but in most real-world situations, the governments and companies will move forward with projects regardless of whether Indigenous groups support it or not. When this happens, due to the legal process and cost involved, there is generally very little that can be done to stop it.

CHAPTER 7

GENOCIDE, CULTURAL GENOCIDE, AND INTERGENERATIONAL TRAUMA

There is a form of violence and oppression called 'cultural genocide,' which is the deliberate attempt to eradicate a specific group by cultural means. This means attempting to eliminate language, spiritual practices, and other traditional ways of life. Assimilation practices carried out by colonial governments are considered cultural genocide. The desire and attempts to eliminate Indigenous culture have been very well documented over the history of colonialism. For example, the "anti-Indian" laws created in the 1800s across North America which forbade Indigenous People from holding culturally significant ceremonies and spiritual practices.

Another strong example of the cultural genocide faced by Indigenous Peoples is the treaties and confinement to living on reserve land. For many Indigenous Nations (though not all), the change of lifestyle from moving freely across a vast territory seasonally to hunt was a cornerstone of the lifestyle and having that altered changed many aspects of traditional culture. Further, it left many nations ill-equipped to lead the new sedentary lifestyle, which led to many issues such as inadequate housing and lack of access to water or food sources.

The "residential schools" were established specifically for the purpose of assimilating Indigenous people into the dominant colonial culture by eliminating the ability for children to learn their Native culture. At the time governments assumed that if they taught Indigenous children in a western way, they would become westernized and assimilate into the settler culture.

According to the Merriam-Webster dictionary, 'genocide' is defined as "the deliberate and systematic destruction of a racial, political, or cultural group" (2014). The overall treatment of Indigenous Peoples in North America unquestionably amounts to a cultural genocide; and sadly, there are many cases where the treatment also amounts to genocide.

Examples of genocidal practices in North

America are not as common as the cultural genocide, which continues to occur to this day. Some argue that genocide must be intentional mass killings of a cultural group, such as what happened in the Holocaust. Certainly, the type of conquering and mass killings carried out in the 1500s by the Spanish conquistadors is genocide. However, practices like withholding access to food in order to either cause death or to pressure a nation into agreeing to and signing a treaty is akin to genocidal practice.

It's hard to imagine the level of racism that Indigenous People have faced, generation after generation, for over 500 years now. It's important to know that this type of trauma compounds and evolves over time and is affecting every aspect of life, making it increasingly difficult for those who are victims of colonial racism and discrimination to take action to change it. It is a multifaceted and extremely complex situation. If we can view the natural world in terms of cause and effect, or equal and opposite reactions, it is likely that however long Indigenous Peoples have been facing this racist discrimination, is how long it would take the future descendants to recover from it.

"Residential and Boarding Schools"

Arguably, "residential schools" have had the most impact on the lives of Indigenous People. Of course, the "schools" were a form of systemic cultural genocide. The fact that this practice was so accepted and systemized shows how deep the anti-Indigenous sentiments were, and how much it has been a part of the mainstream culture in North America.

Shortly after the point of contact, as Europeans were creating more permanent settlements and colonies, various Christian church groups began operating mission schools. These schools were attended by Indigenous children and adults on a voluntary basis. In the early days of European colonialism, many Indigenous Nations worked closely and amicably with the settlers and wanted to learn more of the European languages and culture. In that time, from the early 1600s to the early 1800s, Indigenous People were not forced to attend the mission schools, nor were they expected to discontinue their Indigenous lifestyles if they did so.

In the northern regions of the continent, it was more common for some Indigenous Nations and European settlements to have closer relationships. This led to many Indigenous People marrying settlers and, as mentioned previously, this even created the distinct Métis Nation as a result. At that time, there was a general acceptance of each other's cultures and an openness to cooperate and learn from each other. Many Indigenous People and families chose to go to the mission schools and to partake more in the settler's culture. Due to the Christian education that was taught at the mission schools, many Indigenous People converted to Christianity from that point on, and many still identify as Christian to this day.

Although the mission schools do not have a particularly violent or abusive legacy (although it is entirely possible that mistreatment did occur at these schools as well), many people of Indigenous and European descent still consider them to be overall a part of the practice of cultural genocide as they were intended to alter the culture and belief system of Indigenous People.

It wasn't until after the colonies formed their own distinct nations and governments that "anti-Indian" laws and acts were introduced. At the time, the European colonies and settlements were growing larger and more populous. This led to more conflicts about territory boundaries, land use, and rights and access. The settler and colonial governments of the time believed that the answer to the continuous conflicts would be to eliminate the cultural differences by forcing Indigenous People to assimilate into the dominant culture.

Many laws were created in the 1800s to ban Indigenous cultural practices such as spiritual ceremonies. In an effort to further destroy Indigenous culture and assimilate the people, both the American and Canadian governments decided to take over the school system from the missionaries and created state-run "residential" or "boarding" schools. Children were seized from their homes and moved into the schools, some of which were very far from their Native communities, making it impossible for the families to visit.

Although established through the federal governments, like the mission schools, the so-called "residential" and "boarding schools" were still run by Christian religious institutions such as the Catholic church and other similar organizations.

According to first-hand accounts, and the limited school records, the children who attended the schools were malnourished, lacked access to proper healthcare, and were emotionally, physically, and sexually abused. Many of the children died while in the custody of the schools and the families were never informed of their deaths, the children simply never returned.

Another traumatic impact on Indigenous Peoples that came from the tragic legacy of the "residential" and "boarding schools" was caused by the interruption of family-oriented learning and attachment. The Indigenous children taken from their homes never had the opportunity to be loved and cared for by their families, and thereby also never learned how to love and care for families of their own. The interruption to the social learning of loving and parenting skills occurred repeatedly over generations; parenting skills and socio-family learning were not able to occur for over 150 years.

The multifaceted traumas that the "residential" and "boarding schools" caused have created a deep-seated distrust of all authority and especially colonial power, a depleted sense of self-worth—resulting in many mental health-related illnesses such as depression and substance misuse, the decimation of family skills, learned patterns of abuse—as opposed to learned patterns of care and love, and the list continues from there. With each generation being affected by their own experiences and by the experiences of the generations before them, the legacy and trauma continue.

It was not until 2021 that the yards of the former "residential schools" were excavated and the remains of thousands of children were discovered. Sadly, the remains have been found in mass graves and the children are unmarked and virtually unidentifiable. It may be possible for genetic testing to be done and children to be identified. The remains that are identifiable through matching records are being transported back to their home communities and families so that they may be honored and laid to rest with the dignity and love that they deserve. This goes a long way to helping the families of the missing children, the "residential school" survivors, and the descendants of the "school" survivors get some closure. However, the trauma will take many generations to heal, and that is only if the victims are adequately supported to heal.

CONCLUSION

In the eyes of western science, there is no clear date for when the first people arrived on the continent known as North America today. However, it is clear through both western and Indigenous ways of knowing that they arrived over 15,000 years ago. The mysterious beginning of humanity in North America still motivates archeologists and anthropologists to search for the precise answers of how and when people arrived.

For the better part of the 20th century, the Bering Land Bridge seemed to be the most likely way that people first made their way to North America. It was believed that as the ice, which during the Ice Age covered virtually the entire surface of the Earth, began to recede about 12,000 years ago, people from Siberia were able to walk across the span that separates Asia from North America. This area is now filled with water and called the Bering Strait. According to the Bering Land Bridge theory, the Indigenous Peoples came to North America 12,000 years ago in the North and gradually migrated to the South.

However, it is now believed, though challenging to confirm scientifically, that people were actually able to inhabit the Bering Land Bridge throughout the Ice Age period as well. Furthermore, with more scientific technology becoming available—for example, genetic and chronological testing of remains—it has been confirmed that there were people in North America before the time the Ice Age ended. Tests of remains in many parts of the continent and in South America have proved that there have been people in many parts of the continent as far back as 16,000 years ago.

What is very interesting, and also debunks the Bering Land Bridge theory as the first and only way that people came to inhabit North America, is that genetic tests have confirmed several distinct heritage lines in the remains of the ancient Indigenous Peoples of North America. Archaeological evidence, such as types of tools used in various parts of the ancient Americas, also supports the fact that people in North America have more than one common ancestor.

Many scientists are now convinced that at least some groups of people came to North America by boat following what is called the "Kelp

Highway." The Kelp Highway is the term used to refer to the ancient aquatic ecosystem that flourished along the shoreline that spanned between Asia and North America. It is believed that this thriving ecosystem would have been able to sustain humans as they traveled and explored by sea, eventually landing on the Pacific Coast and dispersing from that arrival point.

Most Indigenous Nations have origin stories that are considered accurate and completely meaningful in terms of needing to know where the people came from. In the Indigenous way of knowing, there is no need for scientific evidence to support the stories; however, in many cases, the scientific evidence is supportive of the origins and creation stories that have been told and retold by Indigenous knowledge keepers since time immemorial.

Whichever way people first came to the Americas is ultimate of little import. What is known is that for thousands of generations, people have evolved in many diverse ways on this continent. Although each Indigenous group is distinct, what is common to all is that they evolved to live in ways that were completely connected with their unique environment and climate. They each evolved in an organic way with the natural world so that the Indigenous way of life was deeply connected with the environment. The Indigenous ways of life were also sustainable and although societal structure evolved to varying degrees over the span of time that people have lived on this continent, each culture and society was sustainable in the environment that it was a part of.

In general, traditional Indigenous cultures and views did not include the concepts of excess or waste, and therefore, many issues that face the western world did not exist; environmental responsibility and stewardship were a natural and integral part of existing. Traditionally, humans tended to view themselves as another form of animal and as a part of the Earth, not as a separate creature that should dominate the environment or the animals. Everything produced and consumed in traditional Indigenous lifestyles came from the Earth and would return to the Earth after its usefulness to the people ended. There was no garbage in the traditional Indigenous ways of living.

Although there are some basic similarities in the lifestyles of Indigenous Nations in North America, there is also an incredible diversity among the cultures. Each Nation and group had its own histories, traditions, ceremonies, and beliefs. Some traditions and ceremonies were shared between neighboring but distinct groups, such as the potlatches of the Pacific Northwest and the Sun Dances of the prairie and northern groups.

Diversity among nations is also observable in the lifestyles of each Nation. Some Indigenous Nations remained nomadic and migrated seasonally up until European contact and even beyond that. Others were agrarian and semi-sedentary or completely sedentary. While others still, like the Zapotecs, had developed elaborate and complex social structures and city-states.

It is important to recognize this diversity and to be aware that not all Indigenous People share the same history and beliefs. In the North American settler popular narrative of Indigenous People's culture and history, there is a common depiction of Indigenous People as having a particular culture, appearance, and customs. This narrative is not accurate or representative of Indigenous Peoples in reality. It is also the narrative that has led to a romanticized and exploitative view of

Indigenous culture, which spreads misinformation about the history of Indigenous Nations, which is both harmful and insulting.

Just as diverse as the cultures and histories of Indigenous Peoples in North America are the contemporary issues that they may or may not face as a result of colonialism. Where some Nations may have had favorable outcomes and are content with their contemporary situation in the context of colonialism and modernity, others may be experiencing many poor outcomes as a result of colonialism. It is also important not to make an assumption of either experience, but to research and possibly ask members of a Nation about the background and the present-day situation and sentiments of the individuals and the Nations.

Although each person and each Nation has had unique experiences, some events have undoubtedly had a grave effect on the majority of Indigenous People in North America and should be approached with the utmost sensitivity, respect, and awareness of the trauma experienced. The "residential" and "boarding schools" are undoubtedly the most impacting colonial practice. With the schools being established in the 1830s and the last school operating up until the 1990s, many victims are still alive and almost every Indigenous person is either a survivor or is a direct relative of a survivor of the "residential" or "boarding schools." In addition to those who have survived, many Indigenous families have stories and memories of the children who never made it home from the "residential" or "boarding schools"; a fate that is so unjust and unimaginable for any parent, sibling, or relative of a missing child to have to accept.

Politically, the Indigenous Nations in North America are in diverse positions as well. Some

Nations live in their traditional territories and have never ceded their claim or right to their ancestral land. Some Nations have treaties that were signed hundreds of years ago, while others still have treaties that were created in the past 50 years. Of these Nations, some are thriving while others may not be regardless of their treaty and status in the eyes of the federal governments. There are many factors that determine the outcomes and well-being of Indigenous Nation communities aside from their political relationship with the settler government and country. Including their own Nation's government and politics as well as the geographic situation of their territory and the access to resources and services that support health and well-being.

Despite the diversity of the politics of each individual nation, there are some overarching issues that many Nations face, and that most Nations collectively accept as affecting

Indigenous Peoples as a whole. The right to sovereignty and self-determination is the most impacting contemporary issue and conflict between Indigenous Nations and settler governments coupled with multi-national companies. This matter has required a loud and dedicated protest over decades to be recognized and heard, and although some progress has been made in the past 20 years or more, it is still an ongoing and hard-fought battle.

Environmental and land use issues are also a major area where Indigenous sovereignty continues to be denied. When companies and governments want to build or extract on ancestral Indigenous lands and territories, there is often little that Indigenous Nations can do to stop them. The legal system, which in the dominating settler culture would be considered the appropriate way to explore the matter of land use and to seek justice, is exclusive and inaccessible to all but those who have deep monetary resources. When the very system allegedly designed to determine what is just and lawful is based on exclusivity and disadvantages those who are not economically able, can it be considered a way to seek justice? This is perhaps a question that is beyond the scope of this book, but in the context of Indigenous Nations and their relationship with settler culture and government, it seems necessary to pose and to reflect upon.

Such documents as FPIC and UNDRIP begin to approach what may be considered justice for Indigenous Peoples worldwide, but have been shown to be weak in practice. Especially when nations and multinational companies may not face any real repercussions for not following the FPIC principles. There is also criticism that even if the principles are respected and followed, they do not go far enough to protect the right to self-determination that Indigenous Peoples are entitled to as a basic human right.

Other contemporary issues worth noting stem from the outcomes that Indigenous People face due to cultural misunderstanding and prejudice on the part of the members of the dominant culture. This leads to assumptions about individuals that may be based on an incorrect portrayal of Indigenous culture in media, in history books, and courses that are written or taught from the western viewpoint.

Another aspect of the misunderstanding of the Indigenous culture is the unrealistic portrayal of Indigenous Peoples and cultures in the media as well as cultural appropriation of Indigenous culture. Many of the books, movies, and TV shows that portray Indigenous People and culture use western stereotypes, which creates a type of caricature of Indigenous people and culture. This is harmful because it reinforces beliefs about Indigenous People that are not true, and it influences the way the members of the dominant culture view Indigenous People.

Cultural appropriation refers to people from a dominant culture using stories, costumes, or other aspects of Indigenous culture as a selling point for their work. This can happen in many forms, for example, Halloween costumes of the westernized concept of the traditional Indigenous dress. These are offensive, as it is demeaning to the culture and to the people to be portrayed as a costume. It also means that a company is profiting off of selling the (inaccurate and demeaning) portrayal of the traditional Indigenous dress. There are several issues here, including that for hundreds of years Indigenous People have been subject to many forms of abuse and prejudice for their cultural practices and have had to fight continuously to maintain the culture. For a company to now be profiting from that is disrespectful to Indigenous People as it is trivializing the entire colonial experience of Indigenous Peoples.

With advocacy and intentional effort to take back control of the narrative of Indigenous culture and history, this is slowly changing. Now more shows, films, and media are being made by Indigenous artists and entrepreneurs. It is always good for non-Indigenous people to consume and support Indigenous artists and their work. By watching shows or movies made by Indigenous filmmakers, non-Indigenous people gain a more accurate understanding of Indigenous culture. Supporting Indigenous artists also means that they will be profiting directly from their work and from representing their culture and perspective, rather than a non-Indigenous person profiting from Indigenous culture.

Although there is a long way to go, for many people this is an important era with newfound hope for reconciliation and healing of colonial wounds and trauma. As non-Indigenous people are becoming increasingly aware of a more accurate history of colonialism in North America, it has broadened the discussion and awareness of the issues and racism that Indigenous Peoples have faced. It is only with true understanding and awareness that reconciliation may begin. It requires a continuous openness to learning and understanding to move past the dark history of colonialism and move forward with respect and dignity for everyone.

REFERENCES

AHA STAFF. (2009, November 16). *Inuit contact: An arctic culture teaching resource.* Perspectives on History. www.historians.org/publications-and-directories/perspectives-on-history/november-2009/inuit-contact-an-arctic-culture-teaching-resource

Asikinack, W. (n.d). *Sun Dance: Indigenous saskatchewan encyclopedia - university of saskatchewan.* Teaching.usask.ca. www.teaching.usask.ca/indigenoussk/import/sun_dance.php

Awali. (2016, November 1). *Democracy and the iroquois constitution.* Field Museum. www.fieldmuseum.org/blog/democracy-and-iroquois-constitution

Bleiweis, S. (2013). *The downfall of the iroquois.* Emory Endeavors in History

2013.
http://history.emory.edu/home/docum
ents/endeavors/volume5/gunpowder-
age-v-bleiweis.pdf

Browner, T. (2019). *Powwow: Native american celebration.* Encyclopædia Britannica. www.britannica.com/topic/powwow

Canadian Museum of History. (n.d.). *Traditional Stories and Creation Stories | Canadian History Hall.* https://www.historymuseum.ca/history-hall/traditional-and-creation-stories/#:~:text=First%20Peoples%20remember%20their%20origins

Carlisle, J. D. (2020, October 20). *TSHA: Choctaw indians.* www.tshaonline.org/handbook/entries/choctaw-indians

Carlysue. (2017, November 8). *Did the indigenous americans take a ride on the kelp highway?* National Geographic

Education   Blog.
blog.education.nationalgeographic.org/
2017/11/08/did-the-first-americans-
take-a-ride-on-the-kelp-highway/

Chesnutt, B. (2021). *Bering land bridge: Evidence & migration.* Study.com. study.com/academy/lesson/bering-land-bridge-evidence-migration.html

Chiblaw, S. (2021, December). *Research framework based on the anishinaabe.* Research   Gate. www.researchgate.net/figure/Research-framework-based-on-the-Anishinaabe-Cree-Medicine-Wheel-Holistic-health_fig1_341257600

Choctaw nation. (n.d.). Heritage & Traditions. ChoctawNation. www.choctawnation.com/history-culture/heritage-traditions

Choctaw tribe. (2012, November 20). WarPaths2PeacePipes.

www.warpaths2peacepipes.com/indian-tribes/choctaw-tribe.htm

Christian, D. (n.d.). Recordkeeping and history. KhanAcademy. www.khanacademy.org/humanities/big-history-project/agriculture-civilization/first-cities-appear/a/recordkeeping-and-history

Clothing. (n.d.) Cree Natives. cree-natives.weebly.com/clothing.html

Colonialism. (n.d.) Indigenouspeoplesatlasofcanada. indigenouspeoplesatlasofcanada.ca/article/colonialism/

Coyle, M. (n.d.). Marginalized by sui generis - duress, undue influence and crown-aboriginal treaties. *Manitoba Law Journal*, vol. 32, no. 2, 2022, p. 34, www.canlii.org/en/commentary/doc/2008CanLIIDocs192#

Cree. (2019, April 6). In *Wikipedia*.

en.wikipedia.org/wiki/Cree

Cross, A. (1990). Raven and the indigenous men from conception to completion.

Cultural traditions of native American hunting and gathering. (2020, April). TribalTrade. tribaltradeco.com/blogs/teachings/cult ural-traditions-of-native-american-hunting-and-gathering

Cultures & traditions: Zapotec (Monte Albán). (n.d.). CollectionsDMA. collections.dma.org/essay/BnlpA3QY

Definition of HOMININ. (n.d.). www.merriam-Webster.com, www.merriam-webster.com/dictionary/hominin

Early human migrations. (2019, May 16). In *Wikipedia*. https://en.wikipedia.org/wiki/Early_hu man_migrations

Erlandson, J. M. (2007, October 30). The kelp

highway hypothesis: marine ecology, the coastal migration theory, and the peopling of the americas. *The Journal of Island and Coastal Archaeology*, vol. 2, no. 2. pp. 161–174, 10.1080/15564890701628612

European contact. (n.d.) Haida History. sites.google.com/site/haidahistory/euro pean-contact

Evans, A. C. (2022). *Zapotec rituals, symbols & animal calendar*. Study. study.com/academy/lesson/zapotec-rituals-symbols-animal-calendar.html

Fen M. (2019, December 18). *The story of how humans came to the americas is constantly evolving*. SmithsonianMag. www.smithsonianmag.com/science-nature/how-humans-came-to-americas-180973739/

Freeman, Milton. (2018). *Arctic indigenous peoples in Canada*.

TheCanadianEncyclopedia. www.thecanadianencyclopedia.ca/en/article/aboriginal-people-arctic

French and iroquois wars (1642-1698). (2019) Uswars. www.uswars.net/french-iroquois-wars/

Gadacz, René R. (2019). *Potlatch*. TheCanadianEncyclopedia. www.thecanadianencyclopedia.ca/en/article/potlatch

Gadacz, René R. (2012, March 7). *Snowshoes*. TheCanadianEncyclopedia. www.thecanadianencyclopedia.ca/en/article/snowshoes

Gadacz, René R. (2021, April 2). *Tipi*. TheCanadianEncyclopedia. www.thecanadianencyclopedia.ca/en/article/tipi

Gardiner, L. (2010). *Inuit culture, traditions, and history*. Windows2Universe. www.windows2universe.org/earth/pola

r/inuit_culture.html

Gibbons, A. (2010). *The human family's earliest ancestors*. SmithsonianMag. www.smithsonianmag.com/science-nature/the-human-familys-earliest-ancestors-7372974/

Gitchi manitou. (n.d.). NativeLanguages. www.native-languages.org/gitchi-manitou.htm

Haida. (n.d.) NewWorldEncyclopedia. www.newworldencyclopedia.org/entry/Haida

Haida the land and the people. (2019). Civilization. www.historymuseum.ca/cmc/exhibitions/aborig/haida/hapso01e.html

Haida tribe. (2017). Warpaths2Peacepipes. www.warpaths2peacepipes.com/indian-tribes/haida-tribe.htm

Hall, A. J. (2017). *Treaties with Indigenous*

peoples in Canada. The Canadian Encyclopedia. www.thecanadianencyclopedia.ca/en/article/aboriginal-treaties

Haudenosaunee guide for educators. (n.d.). Smithsonian Institution National Museum of the American Indian. https://americanindian.si.edu/sites/1/files/pdf/education/HaudenosauneeGuide.pdf

Hiawatha legendary onondaga chief. (n.d.). Britannica. www.britannica.com/topic/Hiawatha

Hileary, C. (2017, June 19). *Native americans call for rethink of bering strait theory.* VOA. www.voanews.com/a/native-americans-call-for-rethink-of-bering-strait-theory/3901792.html

Historic centre of oaxaca and archaeological site of monte albán. (n.d.). UNESCO World Heritage Centre. Unesco.

whc.unesco.org/en/list/415/

Huang, A. (2011). *Totem poles*. IndigenousFoundations.ArtsUBC. indigenousfoundations.arts.ubc.ca/tote m_poles/

Impact of non-indigenous activities on the inuit. (n.d.). Heritage.nf. www.heritage.nf.ca/articles/indigenous/ inuit-impacts.php

Indian Mounds of Mississippi: National Register of Historic Places Travel Itinerary. (n.d.). *Building the mounds*. National Park Service. www.nps.gov/nr/travel/mounds/moun ds.htm

Indigenous peoples of the pacific northwest coast. (2019, October 8). In *Wikipedia*. https://en.wikipedia.org/wiki/Indigeno us_peoples_of_the_Pacific_Northwest _Coast

Johnston, B. (n.d.). The creation story of kitche

manitou (the great spirit) of the ojibwe

Kennedy, D., Bouchard, R., & Gessler, T. (2010, October 24). *Haida*. The Canadian Encyclopedia. https://www.thecanadianencyclopedia.ca/en/article/haida-native-group

Kilroy-Ewbank, L. (n.d.). *Mesoamerica, an introduction*. KhanAcademy. www.khanacademy.org/humanities/art-americas/beginners-guide-art-of-the-americas/mesoamerica-beginner/a/mesoamerica-an-introduction

Kitz, T. (2019, September 26). *Timeline of canadian colonialism and indigenous resistance*. The Leveller. leveller.ca/2019/09/timeline-of-canadian-colonialism-and-indigenous-resistance/

Koehler, S. (2017, September 26). *How environmental racism affects indigenous communities in the USA.* WearYourVoiceMag. www.wearyourvoicemag.com/environmental-racism-affects-indigenous-communities-usa/

Laban Hinton, A. (2014). *Colonial genocide in indigenous north america.* Duke University Press. www.dukeupress.edu/colonial-genocide-in-indigenous-north-america

Little, B. (2020, March 5). *How did humans evolve.* History. www.history.com/news/humans-evolution-neanderthals-denisovans

Mary, L. (2012). *Cree.* FourDirectionsTeachings. www.fourdirectionsteachings.com/transcripts/cree.html

Merriam-Webster. (2014). *Definition of genocide.* Merriam-Webster. www.merriam-webster.com/dictionary/genocide

Merriam-Webster. (2019). *Definition of sovereignty*. Merriam-Webster. www.merriam-webster.com/dictionary/sovereignty

Merriam-Webster. (n.d.). *Definition of time immemorial*. Merriam-Webster. www.merriam-webster.com/dictionary/since%20time%20immemorial

Mitla: The zapotec place of the dead. (2020, December 12). HeritageDaily. www.heritagedaily.com/2020/12/mitla-the-zapotec-place-of-the-dead/136448

Mohawk. (2019). Britannica. www.britannica.com/topic/Mohawk

Morgan, O.L. (2016, August 2). Haudenosaunee (Iroquois) Peacemaking Protocol.

Morlan, R. E. (2006, February 6). *Beringia*. CanadianEncyclopedia.

www.thecanadianencyclopedia.ca/en/ar
ticle/beringia

Native american lands: Ownership and
governance. (n.d.). Revenuedata.
revenuedata.doi.gov/how-revenue-
works/native-american-ownership-
governance/

Native americans describe traditional views of
land ownership. (n.d.). Social History for
Every Classroom. Shec.ashp.cuny.
shec.ashp.cuny.edu/items/show/1543

Native knowledge 360° frequently asked
questions. (n.d.). National Museum of
the American Indian.
americanindian.si.edu/nk360/faq/did-
you-know

Northwest coast native settings. (n.d.).
HistoryMuseum.
www.historymuseum.ca/cmc/exhibition
s/aborig/nwca/nwcam1oe.html

OECD. (n.d.). *Overview of indigenous*

governance in canada: Evolving relations and key issues and debates linking indigenous communities with regional development in canada. OECD-ILibrary. www.oecd-ilibrary.org/sites/b4446f31-en/index.html?itemId=/content/compo nent/b4446f31-en

Parks Canada Agency, G. of C. (2018, February 13). *An Anishinaabe creation story - Pukaskwa National Park.* Www.pc.gc.ca. https://www.pc.gc.ca/en/pn-np/on/pukaskwa/culture/autochtone-indigenous/recit-story

Powell, W. (2012). *Native american creation stories.* Americanyawp. www.americanyawp.com/reader/the-new-world/indian-creation-stories/

Preston, R. J. (2018, May 18). *Nehiyawak Cree.* The Canadian Encyclopedia.

www.thecanadianencyclopedia.ca/en/ar
ticle/cree

Raven Reads. (2018, November 29). *The Raven in Haida Culture*. Raven Reads Books Ltd.
https://ravenreads.org/blogs/news/the-raven-in-haida-culture

Reich, D. (2018). *Clovis people spread to central and south america, then vanished*. HHMI.
www.hhmi.org/news/clovis-people-spread-central-and-south-america-then-vanished

Robinson, A. (2018, April 5). *Trickster*. The Canadian Encyclopedia.
www.thecanadianencyclopedia.ca/en/ar
ticle/trickster

Robinson, A. (2018, March 20). *Vision quest*. The Canadian Encyclopedia.
www.thecanadianencyclopedia.ca/en/ar
ticle/vision-quest

S. Jesse. (2018). *History and future of the book the power of indigenous storytelling.* USask. words.usask.ca/historyofthebook2018/2 018/09/22/the-power-of-indigenous-storytelling/

Saplakoglu, Y. (2019, August 29). *Oldest evidence of north american settlement may have been found in idaho.* Live Science. www.livescience.com/america-settlement-was-by-boat.html

Stinson, J. (n.d.). What are indigenous and western ways of knowing?

Residential schools. (2019, January 14). The Canadian Encyclopedia. www.thecanadianencyclopedia.ca/en/ti meline/residential-schools

The dene nation. (n.d.). *Land of the people.* Dene Nation. denenation.com

The Editors of Encyclopedia Britannica. (2019, January 14). *Iroquois confederacy definition, significance, history, & facts*. Britannica. www.britannica.com/topic/Iroquois-Confederacy

The sun dance sacred ceremony. (2019, December 2). NotesFromTheFrontier. www.notesfromthefrontier.com/post/the-sun-dance-sacred-ceremony

The zapotec world civilization. (n.d.). LumenLearning. courses.lumenlearning.com/suny-hccc-worldcivilization/chapter/the-zapotec/

Tjepkema, M. (2019, December 18). *Life expectancy of first nations, métis and inuit household populations in canada*. Government of Canada, Statistics Canada. StatCan.GC. www150.statcan.gc.ca/n1/pub/82-003-x/2019012/article/00001-eng.htm

Traditional clothing. (n.d.). IndigenousPeoplesAtlasofCanada.

indigenouspeoplesatlasofcanada.ca/arti
cle/clothing/

Traditional medicine: Tobacco. (2021, January
21). CreeHealth. creehealth.org/health-
tips/traditional-medicine-tobacco

Tuttle, R. H. (2019, January 8). *Human
evolution stages & timeline*. Britannica.
www.britannica.com/science/human-
evolution

United Nations Declaration on the Rights of
Indigenous Peoples (n.d.). United
Nations for Indigenous Peoples. UN.
https://www.un.org/development/desa
/indigenouspeoples/declaration-on-the-
rights-of-indigenous-peoples.html

United Nations Department of Economic and
Social Affairs Indigenous Peoples. (2016,
October 14). *Free Prior and Informed
Consent – An Indigenous Peoples' right
and a good practice for local
communities – FAO*. United Nations.

https://www.un.org/development/desa
/indigenouspeoples/publications/2016/
10/free-prior-and-informed-consent-an-
indigenous-peoples-right-and-a-good-
practice-for-local-communities-
fao/#:~:text=FPIC%20is%20a%20princ
iple%20protected

Walker, G. (2016, September 6). *Aztec creation
story*. IndigenousPeople.
www.indigenouspeople.net/aztecs.htm

Zasibley. (2015, February 17). *Potlatch
ceremonies and the repatriation of
potlatch regalia theirs or ours*. Vassar.
pages.vassar.edu/theirsorours/2015/02
/17/potlatch-ceremonies-and-the-
repatriation-of-potlatch-regalia/

OTHER BOOKS BY HISTORY BROUGHT ALIVE

- Ancient Egypt: Discover Fascinating History, Mythology, Gods, Goddesses, Pharaohs, Pyramids, and More from the Mysterious Ancient Egyptian Civilization.

Available now on Kindle, Paperback, Hardcover & Audio in all regions

- Greek Mythology: Explore The Timeless Tales Of Ancient Greece, The Myths, History & Legends of The Gods, Goddesses, Titans, Heroes, Monsters & More

Available now on Kindle, Paperback, Hardcover & Audio in all regions

- Mythology for Kids: Explore Timeless Tales, Characters, History, & Legendary Stories from Around the World. Norse, Celtic, Roman, Greek, Egypt & Many More

Available now on Kindle, Paperback,

Hardcover & Audio in all regions

- Mythology of Mesopotamia: Fascinating Insights, Myths, Stories & History From The World's Most Ancient Civilization. Sumerian, Akkadian, Babylonian, Persian, Assyrian and More

Available now on Kindle, Paperback, Hardcover & Audio in all regions

- Norse Magic & Runes: A Guide To The Magic, Rituals, Spells & Meanings of Norse Magick, Mythology & Reading The Elder Futhark Runes

Available now on Kindle, Paperback, Hardcover & Audio in all regions

- Norse Mythology, Vikings, Magic & Runes: Stories, Legends & Timeless Tales From Norse & Viking Folklore + A Guide To The Rituals, Spells & Meanings of Norse Magick & The Elder Futhark Runes. (3 books in 1)

Available now on Kindle, Paperback, Hardcover & Audio in all regions

- Norse Mythology: Captivating Stories & Timeless Tales Of Norse Folklore. The Myths, Sagas & Legends of The Gods,

Immortals, Magical Creatures, Vikings & More

Available now on Kindle, Paperback, Hardcover & Audio in all regions

- Norse Mythology for Kids: Legendary Stories, Quests & Timeless Tales from Norse Folklore. The Myths, Sagas & Epics of the Gods, Immortals, Magic Creatures, Vikings & More

Available now on Kindle, Paperback, Hardcover & Audio in all regions

- Roman Empire: Rise & The Fall. Explore The History, Mythology, Legends, Epic Battles & Lives Of The Emperors, Legions, Heroes, Gladiators & More

Available now on Kindle, Paperback, Hardcover & Audio in all regions

- The Vikings: Who Were The Vikings? Enter The Viking Age & Discover The Facts, Sagas, Norse Mythology, Legends, Battles & More

Available now on Kindle, Paperback, Hardcover & Audio in all regions

FREE BONUS FROM HBA: EBOOK BUNDLE

Greetings!

First of all, thank you for reading our books. As fellow passionate readers of History and Mythology, we aim to create the very best books for our readers.

Now, we invite you to join our VIP list. As a welcome gift, we offer the History & Mythology Ebook Bundle below for free. Plus you can be the first to receive new books and exclusives! Remember it's 100% free to join.

Scan the QR code to join.

FREE DOWNLOAD

Keep up to date with us on:

YouTube: History Brought Alive

Facebook: History Brought Alive

www.historybroughtalive.com

Printed in the USA
CPSIA information can be obtained
at www.ICGtesting.com
LVHW022339121123
763661LV00008B/252

9 781914 312854